a primer of misbehavior

a primer of

George R. Wesley, Ph. D.

misbehavior

an introduction to abnormal psychology

Nelson-Hall nh Chicago

ISBN 0-911012-21-4

Library of Congress Catalog Card No. 70-185995

To my children:
Lynda, Chuck, Miki, and Sandi

contents

introduction

The word *primer* means any book of elementary principles. This book was conceived for the purpose of teaching the basic concepts of abnormal psychology. Emphasis is placed on a description of the major deviant patterns of behavior. Some conditions are more carefully evaluated than others in accordance with what appears to be important to young people today.

Several words or phrases could have been chosen for the second part of the title, for example, *maladjustment, abnormal psychology,* or *deviant behavior.* Maladjustment was rejected because of the modern concept of adjustment. Most people use this word to mean conformity, and not all nonconforming behavior is bad, nor is all conforming behavior good. Many of the notable advances of mankind have come from people who did not wish to adjust; they wanted to live life to its fullest, to fulfill their potentialities. The word abnormal was rejected largely for the same reason. Abnormal means away from the norm, but this could include the supernormal as well as subnormal.

Many of the things to be discussed in this book are

normal in that everyone behaves in such manner from time to time, or even habitually. But to say they are normal is not to say that they are healthy. In fact, one of the contentions of this book is that most humans waste the bulk of their intelligence in trying to be normal.

The word *misbehavior* was chosen because it means to behave badly. This, in turn, means that some of the things we all do are not good for us simply because they are universal. Nor can we say that all deviant behavior is bad simply because it is unusual. Some behavior patterns labeled as deviant are not truly abnormal; they are merely unusual in certain groups.

One assumption (and it is certainly not the only alternative) of this book is that most misbehavior stems from the twin negative emotions of anxiety and hostility. The overall emphasis is Freudian, but much has to be said about conditioning. In a discussion of anxiety, a psychoanalyst (Freudian) and a conditioning (or behavior) therapist will not drastically disagree in spite of the fact that they often appear at opposite ends.

Several synonyms for anxiety may be used, for example, *fear, dread, apprehension,* and *worry,* but each has slightly different connotations. Dread and apprehension are not widely used in psychological literature, so the major connotative distinction must be made between fear and *anxiety.* But before doing so, it should be helpful to look at the verb worry.

Worry

It is reasonable to assume that most of the worries we have are unrealistic. We worry about things that have already happened when nothing can be done to change them, or we worry about things that could happen but never will, or we worry about letting our parents down when the unreasonable expectations are in our mind, not theirs. We worry about how people will react to us, and the more we worry, the more uncomfortable we make them, so they finally do reject us. We worry about the examination coming up Friday, when if we would stop and reflect, we would know that we have prepared as well as we possibly could. We worry about what a professor thinks of us when he doesn't even know our name. The illustrations could be endless, but they have one thing in common: they are all unfounded apprehensions.

Fear

Fear, like anxiety, dread, worry, and apprehension, is a painful feeling of impending danger, evil, or trouble. But unlike the other terms, fear is realistic. It is anchored to real objects, situations, or events. The fear response is built into our physiological mechanism. Biochemical changes occur within us that help to prepare us to meet an emergency — a response pattern of flight or fight. In ancient times, the fear response enabled man to survive as a species in spite of the fact that man is not the strongest nor the swiftest of animals. Today most of our fears are unrealistic and, therefore, maladaptive. If we do not know the source of our fear, or if the fear is out of proportion to the danger, or if we are misdirected in what we are afraid of, we are experiencing the more generalized version of fear, that is, anxiety.

Anxiety

Anxiety is defined in psychology as a state of apprehension and psychic tension. It differs from fear in that it is more enduring and lasting. The causes are less well defined or not defined at all. According to Freud, there are three basic types of anxiety. These are reality, neurotic, and moral anxiety.

Reality anxiety is similar to fear because what we are afraid of has some basis. There are many objects and situations in the real world that should elicit a fear reaction from us. However, if we sit around and worry about all of the real dangers in the world, we are developing anxiety and are probably beginning to move away from reality anxiety into one of the other types of anxiety. That nuclear power is a danger to all mankind should be a real fear for everyone, but to refuse to leave the cellar because Russia has "the bomb" is taking the reality out of the fear. Some snakes are poisonous and should be feared, but to fear all snakes is unrealistic.

Neurotic anxiety comes closer to the psychological definition of anxiety. In neurotic anxiety we are afraid of one part of ourselves. We are afraid that our emotions are going to get out of control, that we are going to become sexually promiscuous, that we are going to desert our family, or that we are going to punch our boss in the nose. In other words, because we have learned to associate punishment with certain of our actions, we become afraid of some of our own impulses. This type of anxiety, combined with moral anxiety, is at the core of most mental disorders.

Moral anxiety is also a learned fear. The source of moral anxiety is our conscience. Its products are guilt and shame. One part of our personality tells us to do something; another part tells us, "No. That is bad." If we do this thing, we have moral anxiety and feel guilty. If we do not perform this act, we still have psychic tension. This produces neurotic anxiety.

If the ego is strong and healthy, a compromise can be worked out. But if our parents have used excessive punishment to control our behavior, we have little chance of a strong ego. Instead, we have a strong conscience, a conscience that is in a continual state of war with our biological, inherited impulses. The inevitable outcome of this warfare is a weak ego and a continual state of anxiety. We are damned if we do and we are damned if we don't. The internal conflict from this situation weakens our self-esteem and our relationships with others. This, in turn, creates more problems in the external world. The increased problems increase our anxiety. We can't win. We have to find a way to get off this merry-go-round. Most people do find a way, but few find a happy, productive escape.

In this discussion of anxiety, the terms *id, ego,* and *superego* are often employed. It would be helpful to clarify these concepts at this point.

Id

Freud postulated three structures of personality: the id, the ego, and the superego. The id is man's biological inheritance. It is the "I want" aspect of personality. It is *asocial* in that it has no regard for other people. Its purpose is to seek pleasure and to avoid pain. It works on the principle, "I want what I want when I want it without regard for anyone else." The id cannot be called antisocial; neither can it be called social. It is totally unrealistic in any social sense. Rank hedonism is its purpose. Some id impulses can be satisfied without hurting other people; others cannot. In other words, civilization has properly imposed some limits on man's nature. Raw aggression cannot be condoned in any civilized society even if this type of drive may be the very impulse that enabled *Homo sapiens* to survive as a species.

The reasons for the large number of prohibitions that

are imposed on one other id impulse, sex, are not as easy to see. Nevertheless, almost all of the world's societies have some restrictions on the expression of the sexual impulses. In the United States the prohibitions against sex are quite severe.

If man is to survive as a species, there must be some provision in any civilization for the expression of the sexual and aggressive drives. Therefore, a child has to be taught the circumstances under which these impulses can be expressed. This socialization is the major responsibility of any parent and, sooner or later, the values of the parents become one dimension of the child's personality. Thus, an ego begins to develop in the child.

Ego

The ego may be described as the "reality principle." Its purpose is to postpone, to delay, to rearrange, to compromise, to mediate, or to arbitrate. All of these things are done to give man a social responsibility. Some pleasures can be greater if they are postponed. Many needs cannot be satisfied without the help of other people. Goals give a man's life meaning and an immeasurable amount of pleasure. Therefore, immediate gratification can and frequently does work to an individual's disadvantage rather than to his advantage. For example, if we gave vent to our id impulses in their raw form, it is unlikely that any of our children would survive infancy.

Superego

But what does the ego mediate between? The ego becomes the arbitrator between the id and the superego. The superego has been described as a sort of inner mother, through which the restrictions of a society become internalized. Since mothers are usually the closest representative of the society to the child, it is reasonable to attribute superego formation to the mother in most cases. The infant knows nothing about the total society. He learns what to expect from the culture by way of his mother or mother substitute. If the mother is punitive, the superego is going to become punitive. If the mother is indulgent, the superego will be indulgent (in some cases too indulgent).

The superego is composed of two components, the conscience and the ego ideal. The conscience is the "no" aspect of personality. When the conscience says "no," it means absolutely "no." This is an absolute prohibition or restriction. Therefore, the conscience is just as unrealistic as the id. The "Thou shalt not" of the conscience is a final answer. It cannot compromise.

On the other hand, the mother's positive values can also become a part of the child's personality. These are incorporated into the structure which Freud called the ego ideal. This becomes the "I should, I ought to, I must" dimension of personality. The goals, ambitions, aspirations, and ideals of an individual are included in this system. Once in a while the ego ideal causes a person trouble; when a person has unreasonable aspirations, he may become very frustrated, bitter, and cynical by his failure to achieve these goals. However, the real villain of personality is the conscience.

Almost every so-called abnormal person whom a psychologist sees is an individual with an overdeveloped conscience. These people live in a world of "don'ts," but the restrictions are mostly internal rather than external. They live in a constant state of anxiety because every time they turn around they have done something that their conscience says is wrong. Their every thought and action produce feelings of guilt and shame.

Punishment and hostility

When parents employ punishment as their primary technique for controlling children, they are concentrating on conscience formation. They want and ultimately get internal control, but they fail to realize that the "inner mother" cannot reason. It can never logically deduce that there is a time, a place, and a situation in which the "no" might possibly become a "yes." Therefore, when the child grows up and enters the real world, he cannot make the adjustment to reality because of the total unreality of a conscience that is too punitive.

The relationship between anxiety and hostility can now be established. Fear is to anxiety as anger is to hostility. Like fear, anger is adaptive and realistic. Also, like fear, it is a built-in response brought about by physiological changes within the body. Once more, the body is getting prepared for action—an action that may save the life of the individual. There are times when it is totally realistic and even constructive to become angry.

The more generalzied version of anger, that is, hostility, grows out of the tendency of many parents to try to repress all aggression. Thus, we meet anger in the child by becoming aggressive ourselves; we resort to punishment as the means of controlling the child's behavior. After many years of studying the effects of punishment on animals and humans, psychologists can say no more than, "the results of punishment are unpredictable." Sometimes it works the way we want it to work; sometimes it works in the opposite direction. Even when it has the desired effect, there are side effects which are uncontrollable. These by-products are mostly negative.

One by-product of punishment is the attachment of aversive qualities to previously neutral stimuli. For example, if a child is frequently punished in his room, everything in the room acquires secondary (learned) aversive characteristics. The parents then wonder why the child fights going to bed in this room. The child stalls as long as possible and when he finally does go to bed there is a strong possibility that he will irritate his parents even more by staying awake too long. Why? Punishment has been associated with the room and the objects in the room. If punishment is to work, it must be associated with the act in time and place. The longer punishment is delayed, the less predictable the outcome is going to be. In fact, the punishment may become associated with a desirable act.

Punishment and anxiety

Another by-product of punishment is anxiety. When a child is punished, he loses some of his security because he feels, at one level or another, that if he were truly loved he would not be the victim of wrong. This anxiety leads to a multitude of other feelings. He feels defenseless because he is so much smaller than his adversary. He feels guilty because he has done something "bad" which led to a loss of love; he feels helpless because he cannot fight back. All of these feelings are unpleasant and extremely uncomfortable.

When one experiences this degree of discomfort, it is only natural that he become angry. Thus, the original anxiety can, and usually does, lead to hostility. But, as already pointed out, many parents absolutely prohibit any attempt on the part of the child to fight back. The anger has to be repressed; it is forced to remain in the unconscious where it can build day by day into potentially explosive hostility. In later years, we lose any awareness of the storehouse of hostility that we all must have toward our parents. But, of course, hostility can be expressed in a thousand different ways. A few examples are verbal assault and rejection, negativism, resistance to all authority, competition, and open aggression.

Freudians and behaviorists agree on at least one point. Inappropriate anger and fear are negative emotions which can lead to some severe consequences. The neo-behaviorists, especially Skinner (1953), have presented a strong case against punishment as an effective means of controlling behavior. In spite of this, it is doubtful that punishment is going to be abandoned any time in the near future. Why? Punishment is easy. A fool can wait until an inappropriate act occurs and then try to stop any further occurrence of the behavior by punishing. This technique requires about as much ingenuity as putting on a pair of loafers. Instilling a positive set of values requires thinking, and thinking is work (at times it can even be painful).

Another reason that punishment will be around for a long time is the Christian assumption that man is evil. This premise shows up in the attitude of most parents. "He is going to hell, if I don't beat the hell out of him." The reasoning seems to be that if man is inherently evil, there is only one way to deal with him – scare or punish him into being good. In fact, the best way to scare "the devil" out of him is to threaten him with eternal punishment. When this assumption is made, it logically follows that punishment becomes the manner for dealing with children, social deviants, and heretics of any other type. Punishment becomes a way of life as well as a philosophy of life.

Where a priori assumptions of this type run into trouble is that they are untestable. There is no way to prove the "goodness" or "evilness" of man except by way of post ad hoc deductions. If we look at modern man, we find much evidence to support the conclusion that man is inherently evil. However, how much misbehavior can be traced to the way people were handled as children?

The Role of Sex

The role of sex in the etiology of misbehavior cannot be overestimated. Almost every patient in a mental hospital has sexual and/or religious hang-ups. Americans, in comparison with other peoples, are rather strict in their attitudes and teaching about sex. Many children, especially girls, are taught that sex is sinful, wicked, shameful, dirty, vulgar, or common. They are taught, "Don't do it until you are married." The triple threats of infection, conception, and detection are used to imply dire and tragic consequences. Sometimes even parents who are conscientious and thoughtful in all other ways impose their feelings of guilt and shame on their children.

Thorpe et al. described the situation as follows:

> The parents' feelings of shame and disgust are displayed in a variety of manners and patterns. A frown, a wince, a gasp all have their effect on the impressionable young child. The total impression on the child is that there is something wrong with sex. The infant, for example, is being changed on the bassinet. Random activity may cause him to place his hand on his genitals. Quick as a flash, his mother removes his hand. If the child should persist in keeping it there, mother may slap his hand. If the child's hand touched any other part of his body, nothing would happen. The child is being taught: You must never touch your genitals.
>
> These parental attitudes continue to influence the child as he matures. The child of two is usually taught to learn to name the parts of his body. Every part of the body is mentioned and named except his genitals. Again he is being taught: You must never mention your genitals. At three he is reminded to "put something on." He is being taught: You must never show your

genitals. At four he usually asks about where babies come from. Very often he is ignored. He is being taught: You must never discuss sex. At five he may be apprehended in sex play with a sibling or playmate. He is usually severely reprimanded. He is being taught: You must never show any active interest in sex. (Louis P. Thorpe, Barney Katz, and Robert T. Lewis, *The Psychology of Abnormal Behavior—A Dynamic Approach*, 2nd ed. New York: Ronald Press Co., 1961, p. 169.)

These attitudes continue into middle childhood and adolescence through the conversation and actions of the parents. Even marriage is not enough for many people to overcome all of the indoctrination they have received from their parents, relatives, peers, and church.

Unacceptable impulses have to be kept out of our consciousness. This process is called repression and is one of the defense mechanisms. It is to these mechanisms, our first line of defense, that we now turn.

1
defense mechanisms

The easiest, most normal way to break the vicious sex-anxiety-hostility circle is to develop defense mechanisms, or dynamisms as they are sometimes called. As the name implies, these are mental mechanisms which protect (defend) or enhance our ego. Their purpose is to cloud what is real, and even to hide parts of ourselves from us. They make it almost impossible for us to see ourselves as others see us. They allow us to have "pure" motives, to be good and honorable, to be persecuted, and to be a critic of other people. It has been said that all men would like to be God, but a few never realize that this is impossible. Defense mechanisms help us to become little deities, at least unto ourselves.

On the other hand, it would be a mistake to label defense mechanisms as abnormal, for they are not. Everyone uses them at times, and most people use them continuously. Mental mechanisms are not all bad. They help people to live with themselves and, at times, even to like themselves. If one cannot live with himself, he will find it difficult to live with anyone else. The same can be said of liking himself.

Defense mechanisms become dangerous when the real world becomes an imaginary world, when self-esteem becomes narcissism, when nothing is our fault, when misery replaces happiness, and when we cannot come anywhere close to accepting ourselves as we really are. Defense mechanisms border on the dangerous when we have a rational reason for everything we do, when we become name-callers, when we show exaggerated behavior of any type, when we wall off our emotions and refuse to participate in life, or when we spend most of our time trying to forget.

Repression

This mechanism underlies all of the other defense mechanisms. If we are aware of what we are doing when we protect or enhance our ego, the dynamisms lose some of their effectiveness. Repression is the unconscious forcing of dangerous ideas, memories, or perceptions into the unconscious. Unconscious was purposely used twice in this definition. If we are conscious of the fact that we are trying to forget something, the mechanism is not repression, but suppression. In repression, any painful experience is pushed out of awareness into the reservoir of the unconscious. This allows us to forget the pain, but the experience remains active at the unconscious level, that is, our future behavior is guided by this dangerous and/or painful memory, although we are unaware of the motivation.

The old adage, "Time is the great healer," may not be as accurate as we would like it to be. We may forget how many times our parents beat us when we were an infant and child, but these memories linger on to guide our future behavior, not only with our parents, but with all people. We repress the pain, but it is still there in the unconscious. We may react to all people with an expectation of being hurt and we will find our predictions to be fulfilled, because humans are in the habit of living up to our expectations. Any act they perform is capable of being good or evil. Whether the act is bad or good depends to a large extent upon how we perceive it. Good and evil are not inherent in nature; they are value judgments made by human beings.

Repression also works to keep various impulses, attitudes, and beliefs at the unconscious level. Id impulses are buried below the level of awareness. These impulses are never allowed to come to the surface, because if they did, we would consider ourselves evil through and through. This would be too painful for us to accept. After a person has developed language, that is, consciousness, all id impulses come to consciousness via the ego. This means that by the time we become aware of something, it has already been compromised. We are the good, the pure, the honorable, the saintly. Everyone else is possessed by the devil and the evil spirits.

Superego components are also largely repressed. We like to think that we are normal, that we don't have any abnormal inhibitions or prohitibions. An instance of superego repression occurs when a girl who has been told all her life that sex is dirty, vulgar, filthy, evil, a sin, gets married. She feels that her attitude toward sex is normal and natural. As soon as she is married, everything will be well. For a few weeks or months things are fine because her desire to give, her pleasure in making her husband happy, and the excitement of satisfying long-delayed emotions overshadow the feelings of repulsion and guilt that she has about sexual relations with anyone.

Sooner or later, the unconscious or conscious battle

between the id and the superego begins to show up in her behavior. She becomes less interested in pleasing her husband and more interested in going to sleep. She begins to find excuses for not having intercourse with her husband: she is too tired, too sleepy, too "keyed up," or too upset; she doesn't feel well; intercourse hurts; the day was too hectic. These rationalizations satisfy the punitive superego and, at the same time, allow her to keep her self-concept of normality. "After all," she will say, "there's more to marriage than just sex. Sometimes I think my husband is little better than an animal."

Suppression

This dynamism is very similar to repression except that when we use this mechanism, we consciously or deliberately try to forget. Painful or dangerous memories, ideas, or perceptions are pushed out of our awareness in a hundred ways. We read, work, play cards, go to movies, indulge in sports, watch television, or engage in any number of other activities. These activities may be worthwhile in themselves, but when they are employed to suppress they take on an almost narcotic quality. It is quite easy to find people in any town with "bridgitis," "golfitis," TVitis," or "movieitis." These people are addicted to an activity. They spend most of their waking hours in some activity that will help them forget.

If we have a problem in life and ask the amateur psychologists for advice, their usual answer is, "Occupy yourself. Stay busy. Try to forget about it." This advice fails to take into account the probable conversion of suppression into repression. When we truly forget, that is, when we repress, we can no longer remember the pain, but it is still with us nevertheless. It becomes a part of our unconscious motivation and remains active enough to guide our future behavior. Hence, if the repressed material resulted from a painful experience with a boy friend or a girl friend, we enter into any boy-girl relationship with motives of which we are totally unaware.

These unconscious attitudes affect our new relationships in many ways, most of which are negative. We are frequently unhappy in the new situation, but we cannot find the reason why. We have been successful in forgetting the pain and the hurt, but we have done so by burying part of our personality.

Identification (introjection)

This is a normal process, within limits. This dynamism enables the infant to become a social being. By incorporating into his personality the attitudes, beliefs, and characteristics of others, the child becomes a unique individual himself. Usually the child acquires the mores, customs, habits, opinions, and prejudices of those closest to him. Because the mother, under normal circumstances, is the person who has most contact with the child, the value system of the child is frequently almost identical to that of his mother. If the mother's conscience is a restrictive tyrant, the child's conscience will probably be overdeveloped. To a lesser degree, the child identifies with his father and other people in his environment. Therefore, the ultimate personality of an individual depends upon a "taking in" from many people.

Thus far, the discussion of identification has been concerned with a normal variety. The major way that problems can be created in this process is for our models to be inappropriate. About one-third of the men in prison today can be classified as dyssocial, that is, they learned their behavior in a normal way, but their models were antisocial or asocial. These men are not abnormal in relation to their group; they are only different when compared with the total society. They simply learned behavior which deviates from the cultural norms. A neurotic or prejudiced parent can cause his children to have the same characteristics.

Identification can be used as a defense mechanism. When one parent is feared, one of the easiest ways the child can reduce the threat is to become so much like the strict parent that he is no longer an anxiety-producing object. A child is more likely to become like a feared parent than he is a loved parent. In identification, anxiety reduction seems to overshadow love.

Not only do children behave in this manner, but so do adults. A short look into history shows many Germans reducing the Hitler threat by identifying with his programs. According to Erikson (1950), Germans were accustomed to this type of identification because of the rigid authoritarian structure of the typical German family. Hitler merely became the feared father figure. The easiest way to reduce the threat was to become like the image. Many members of minority groups employ the same type of identification for the same purpose. If one can become like members of the majority group, one no longer feels threatened by them.

Vicarious living can be another type of identification. This can be adjustive or non-adjustive depending upon the circumstances and the frequency. To go to the movie and cry shows that we have feelings for others; we are capable of empathy and sympathy. But to become addicted to movies because our real world is too painful or unpleasant is probably dangerous because our identification is taking us into a fantasy world. To identify so closely with a movie star that we imitate his every action, mannerism, and hair style is probably an admission that we prefer the dream-world to the real world. Much the same can be said with regard to reading or watching television. When a habit has us instead of our having it, we are likely to have severe problems or anxiety. We can lose our own identity by identifying too closely with others.

To have known many great people is satisfying. To become name-droppers is an admission that the only way we can make ourselves great is to hope that some of the reputation of great people will rub off on us. This is especially obvious when we resort to the habit of referring to world-renowned people by their first names.

Not only do we identify with people; we can and do identify with groups or institutions. A Marine is expected to lose much of his personal identity. He is not allowed to forget that he is a Marine first, and John Doe second. One large measure of the "spirit" on any college campus is the degree of identification the students show toward the school. It is ego-inflating to say, "We won the football game," even if the extent of our participation was to listen to the game on the radio.

Any one of these types of identification can be kept within a normal range. Any one of them can be used to protect and enhance our ego.

Displacement

This is the mechanism by which psychic energy is rechanneled from one object, person, or situation to another. The name assigned to a type of displacement depends largely upon the impulse involved.

When hostility or aggression is the impulse to be dealt with, displacement is called scapegoating. This mechanism involves transferring our hostility to someone or something else. A feared person or a person in a position of authority over us makes us angry. Instead of becoming aggressive toward this person, we hold back the emotion, go home, and take it out on the children. The children are not responsible for our pent-up emotions, but since they are non-threatening, they are the logical choice of someone against whom we can vent our hostility. The term scapegoating is derived from the old Biblical practice of symbolically laying the sins of the people on the head of a goat which was then driven into the wilderness. This is exactly what we do when we use this defense mechanism. We make some innocent person, animal, or object into the goat.

Since all societies have to deal with aggression, one measure of the potential mental health of a culture is the extent to which the members can find safe scapegoats. People are poor scapegoats because they, too, can become aggressive. Animals can have the same disadvantage. This leaves objects as the most logical choice. Contact sports have great release value for the participants, but there is always the danger that aggression may get out of hand because people are involved. Noncontact sports should be encouraged because they are ideal object scapegoats. A bowling pin or golf ball rarely if ever hits back. Any physical activity helps to reduce anger because this feeling is at least partly physiological in origin.

America has many so-called safe channels for relieving aggressive emotions, but most of these are potentially dangerous. Competition in school or the business world is not only condoned, it is encouraged. Boxing, football, and wrestling are among our most popular sports. War seems like a national institution.

Organized persecution and prejudice against minority groups is perfectly acceptable to a segment of the American population. In fact, a good illustration of the scapegoat value of discrimination is reflected in the inverse relationship between the price of cotton and the number of lynchings in the deep South a few decades ago.

The automobile works effectively as a tension reducer for many individuals, but the danger of this 3000-4000-pound weapon is becoming more and more apparent in the highway death and injury statistics.

In Japan today one industry provides a therapy room. Employees are given as much time off with pay as they need to work off their hostility. Destructible objects, baseball bats, and even dummies of the bosses are provided. The employee can beat the dummy of his boss for a solid hour if he so desires. This is the type of outlet the United States should start experimenting with. We need safe scapegoats, not the quasi-safe outlets that we have today. A child needs destructible toys, objects that will take a sound beating, and an attitude of competition with himself, not with others. Aggression may be a part of man's nature, but it does not necessarily have to be vented on his fellow man.

When there are no outlets for aggressive emotions, the hostility can turn inward on the person experiencing the emotion. This is a situation which produces psychosomatic disorders, such as ulcers and migraine headaches, and is the major underlying cause of depressive reactions.

Compensation

A second type of displacement is compensation which involves a real or an imagined deficiency. It seems to matter little whether or not a handicap is real; most individuals react in much the same manner. There are several ways we can compensate. One is to redouble our efforts to overcome the deficiency. For example, if we don't make the first team in football, we can practice, practice, practice until we overcome our lack of native ability.

A friend of the author's, as a child, was clumsy and slow. He wanted to become a great football player, so he compensated. Every afternoon he could be found kicking and punting a football. He became a high school star, went through college on a full four-year scholarship, and is now a coach at a large American university. All of this was made possible by his "educated toe." In other respects he is not a great deal more coordinated today than he was as a child.

Another way we can compensate is to accept a substitute goal. This goal may remain similar to the original, for example, we may become a great baseball player or a walking encyclopedia of sports statistics instead of a football star; or the goal may be far removed from the original, for instance, we may become a straight A student.

Compensation employed as suggested above is probably helpful to the individual and can be quite helpful to society. Psychologists are not too concerned about compensation until it becomes overcompensation. When the mechanism reaches this extreme, the person's behavior is usually exaggerated. At this time compensation can become dangerous. For example, extremely small men frequently develop what is known as the Napoleonic complex. They overcompensate for their size by becoming overly aggressive and belligerent. They are at war with the world of the larger person. Lower their inhibitions just slightly, as with alcohol, and they are ready to fight (usually the biggest man in the room). If they become college professors, they are so perfectionistic that students find them almost unbearable. These men are miserable themselves, and make life miserable for everyone around them.

A usual characteristic of people who have to become extremists in an effort to protect and enhance their egos is a sensitivity to any criticism about the thing they are fighting. Therefore, if someone makes a reference to the sensitive area, these people lose control of their emotions and overreact in a negative manner. Only extremely tolerant and patient people will condone this type of behavior for long. The usual outcome is that the overcompensator alienates other people, and this alienation, in turn, agitates his feeling of deficiency or inadequacy. He has to try (compensate) that much more to overcome the problem. This alienates more people. He is caught in another of those infamous vicious circles.

It has been said that everyone has an inferiority complex except those individuals with a superiority complex, and a superiority complex is merely a cover for very strong inferiority feelings. This could illustrate another type of overcompensation that creates an alienation circle. Continual bragging about oneself does not generally win one friends.

Compensation frequently enters into our statements about other people. The empirically observed positive relationships between intelligence and success, popularity, strength, stature, and physical appearance are often ignored in popular statements about others. If a person has one advantage we resent the fact that he may have many advantages. Thus, we say, "Beautiful, but dumb." "All brawn, no brain." "Bookworm." "Dumb blonde."

Gossip is another way to compensate for our real or imagined inadequacies. We can reduce others to our size by slander and gossip. This allows us to enhance and protect our ego because, after character defamation, others have limitations and defects equal to our own. The exaggeration that usually accompanies compensation is readily seen in gossip. The more limitations a person imagines he has, the more likely he is to indulge in petty, malicious gossip. Nothing delights people more than a scandal involving some famous public figure.

Sublimation

According to Freud's definition, sublimation is the rechanneling of sexual energy into a socially acceptable activity. Many psychologists say that if we have to use a defense mechanism, this is the one to use because of its value to society. They refer to notable historical figures who probably had a limited sex life, or no sex life, and relate their accomplishments to a frustrated sex drive.

The idea is that the tensions which arise out of frustrated id impulses have to be released, and we might as well employ this energy in a socially constructive manner. We can become motivated to write, to build bridges or buildings, to sing, to paint, to help the poor, or to invent. Freud (1947) cites Leonardo da Vinci as a classical example of a person who must have used sublimation as a major defense against his latent homosexuality. Freud felt that da Vinci was largely asexual throughout his life and that he chanelled his repressed sexual energy into his scientific and artistic endeavors.

There is some question as to how much an individual can sublimate. Certainly it is possible for a person to live an entire life without sex. Sex is probably a relatively weak biological drive. It is not necessary for an individual to survive, although it is necessary for species survival. If sex is biologically weak, the preoccupation of Americans with sex can probably be traced to psychological-social conditioning. This obsession is one form of substitution.

Substitution

In sublimation, there is actually a change in goals. Sexual energy is rechanneled to some object that has no direct relation to sex. A more probable redirection of this energy is covered by the defense mechanism called substitution. When this dynamism is employed, the goal, that is, sexual satisfaction, remains the same. However, rather than direct satisfaction of the sex drive, the person finds some substitute satisfaction. The rechanneling is only marginally acceptable to society, and in some instances it is totally unacceptable.

One marginal substitution in America today is masturbation. Very few adults today try to frighten children into abstaining from this autoerotic activity. Neither do they approve of or condone this practice. Instead they turn their heads and pretend that masturbation does not exist.

Another marginal substitution is the partial satisfaction of sex vicariously through magazines or books. It seems all a current author has to do is to include a sex scene in his book to make it a best seller. One can take one look at the magazines on any book rack and immediately tell just how much substitution goes on in America. Movies and television are peddling sex to the public at an equally rapid pace. Many advertisers have stressed sex in recent years. All of these people know which side their bread is buttered on. They know the sickness that is a part of the personality of many Americans.

Sexual deviation is a type of substitution which is unacceptable to a majority of the American public. That

so-called abnormal sex is emotionally charged is reflected in sodomy laws which make this a "heinous
crime against God and nature." The sodomy laws are
so vaguely worded that what constitutes a crime can be
almost anything. Some states make "heavy petting" a
crime. If this law were enforced in these states, much of
the population would be behind bars. Another "heinous,
unnatural act against God and man" is mouth-genital
contact, practiced by more than sixty percent of all
college graduates. When the ratio reaches this proportion, how can it be called abnormal? Yet the substitution
value of other types of behavior, such as pyromania and
kleptomania, goes almost unnoticed.

Sexually deviant people are rarely oversexed. Very
few of them are maniacs or fiends. Contrary to popular
belief, they are usually people with very strong prohibitions and inhibitions against normal sex. As with most
abnormal people, they have an overdeveloped conscience. Deviancy is simply less threatening to them than
are normal sexual relations. What, then, do we accomplish by putting them in prison?

To complicate matters even more, our prisons are
breeding grounds for homosexuality. These so-called
abnormal people are probably little different from the
frequenters of the burlesque shows, the attendants at
the male "smokers," the avid collectors of pornographic
literature, or even the local censors (after all, a censor
has to read what he censors).

Intellectualization

An effective way to rid ourselves of emotions is to
attach them to our intellect, thereby eliminating the
emotional charge. This process is called intellectualization. Some people can say, "I hate my mother," as

though they were saying, "It's a nice day." They have intellectualized their emotions to such an extent that there is little or no feeling left. We can intellectualize in several ways.

Rationalization is one of these. This mechanism is defined as giving a socially acceptable reason for an action. Basically, it is excuse-giving. Americans literally teach their children to rationalize by continually asking them, "Why did you do such-and-such?" If a child comes up with a good excuse, he is reinforced by not being punished. If he told the truth — "Because I hate you" — the odds are strong that he would not say this too many more times. By the time children reach adolescence, they have become so proficient in excuse-giving that they have a ready-made excuse for almost everything they do. They are not lying; they are telling the truth as they see it. They have completely hidden their real reasons from themselves.

It is amazing how many people can rationalize almost anything by being sick or "feeling bad." This can become a prefabricated excuse for failure of any type, whether it be in school, in business, in marriage, or in interpersonal relationships. "My health held me back." "What is wrong?" you may ask. The answer: "I don't know; I just don't feel good."

A widespread rationalization among young women today is the "love" rationalization. In contrast to their parents, the girls of this generation feel that sex is fine as long as they are in love. They do not have to wait for marriage. Love is the suitable excuse.

There are two basic types of rationalization. The first is called *sour grapes*. The model for this mechanism is the story of the fox in Aesop's *Fables* who kept trying to reach some grapes. He tried everything he could think of but still failed. Finally, he walked away saying,

"Oh well, they were sour anyhow." This is what we do when we use the sour grapes mental mechanism. A college student flunks out of college. Does he accept the blame? Does he admit that he was lazy and stupid? Of course not. He says, "It wasn't worth it anyhow. Anyone who stays in *that* college must be dumb." A bridegroom is left standing at the altar. He says, "How did I ever get involved with that stupid broad? I should have known better."

The other major type of rationalization is called *sweet lemons*. This is that grand old philosophy of not doing what you like, but forcing yourself to like what you do. Within limits, this mechanism is reasonable, because society places some restrictions on what every one of us does or can do. We may not like to wear clothes, but we have to if we are to remain in the mainstream of society. If every unhappily married couple obtained a divorce, the divorce statistics would skyrocket.

This type of defense mechanism can become dangerous when we are so successful that our real feelings become hidden. This allows us to refuse to recognize that we even have a problem. But if Freud is right, the material remains active at the unconscious level and is there to guide our behavior. The man who has to rationalize an insignificant job into significance is very unlikely to be a good husband or father. Staying together for the sake of the children may defeat the purpose.

Suppression and sweet lemons rationalizations frequently go hand-in-hand. Not only does the individual have to continually talk himself into liking what he is doing, but he also probably has to stay busy to forget. Or he may use the sleep escape. His life is so full of problems and unhappiness that he has to get away. What safer way is there to escape than to sleep? After all, what trouble can one get into while he is asleep?

Compartmentalization (isolation) is a second type of intellectualization. This is a process of forming logic-tight mental compartments. Contradictory attitudes are psychologically walled off so that they will not interfere with one another. The person has no idea that he has a multitude of attitudes that are diametrically opposed to one another.

This mechanism is illustrated by statements such as "All criminals should be lynched," and "It is our Christian duty to keep those Negroes out of our church." People whose thinking is compartmentalized can make statements of this nature without recognizing the contradiction. They feel that they are consistent and would probably react violently if the inconsistency were pointed out to them. Prejudiced people frequently employ this mechanism as well as one that Allport (1958) called re-fencing. In re-fencing, the person hastily admits any exception to his system and then promptly forgets that this exception ever existed. For example, if an individual is prejudiced against Negroes, he will readily accept the pseudoscientific proofs that Negroes have inferior intelligence. When he meets an intelligent Negro, this experience is promptly repressed as it does not fit into his logical system.

Undoing is a third type of intellectualization. This mechanism involves doing something positive to offset something negative that has already occurred. For example, a husband steps out on his wife, and then brings some flowers home to her. Undoing is a type of cleansing ritual which, when exaggerated, can become a compulsion, for example, a washing compulsion. This dynamism is probably not very effective because when we suddenly become too nice, other people are frequently suspicious of our motives. They wonder what we have been up to. On the other hand, we can purge ourselves of much guilt by making a concerted effort to be nice.

Emotional insulation is the fourth and the final type of intellectualization. This defense takes the form of psychologically walling off our emotions. If we have been hurt, it is probably only natural that we become a little gun-shy. However, if we build a wall around our emotions, we are blocking the positive emotions as well as the negative ones. We miss much of living when this type of intellectualization takes place.

Apathy is viewed as a danger sign by most psychologists because it means we have given up the fight. Our emotional problems have produced so much and such prolonged conflict that we withdraw into a psychological shell. Once withdrawn, we don't live, we merely exist. Within the shell, battles are still being waged. Therefore, apathetic people can, and frequently do, explode.

Projection

This mechanism can be called a type of displacement or a type of intellectualization because it is both. Usually though, it is listed by itself, not under either classification. In projection, a person attributes his own characteristics to others. Almost always, these projected impulses are undesirable to the individual. His conscience will not allow him to have this type of feeling. For example, "I hate you" becomes "You hate me." When this transformation has occurred, I can justify my aggression toward you because I am only defending myself. How often are enemy soldiers accused of bestiality, brutality, and sexual aberrations during a time of war?

Homosexuality is a characteristic which is often projected. When repression is complete, homosexuality becomes latent. Then the individual begins to accuse others of having this tendency. He may become malicious in his gossip about other persons. He may go out on frequent "queen hunts." He picks up a homosexual and then assaults him. He may ridicule men who have effeminate traits. Under any circumstance, one part of his own personality remains extremely sensitive because he is a constant combatant with himself to keep the tendency repressed. For this reason, latent homosexuals can be, and sometimes are, dangerous. To remind this person of his repressed tendency is to chance inciting a psychological explosion. A woman who threatens this person's male ego, intentionally or inadvertently, is taking her life into her hands. Latent homosexuals may be described as mobile powder kegs. Many psychologists see projected latent homosexuality as the underlying dynamic cause for paranoia.

Prejudice and projection are closely related. Most stereotypes about minority groups include sexual and aggressive statements. Some examples of the accusations against various subgroups in America are: knife carrying, hotheaded, whiskey-drinking, lazy, and sexually promiscuous. The problem for members of a minority group is that you are damned if you do, and damned if you don't. If Jewish people do not compensate, bigots call them lazy, good-for-nothing bums. If they do compensate, and achieve, they are accused of a Jewish conspiracy, a take-over of the country.

Reaction formation

This defense mechanism is a near relative of projection. It is defined as doing just the opposite of what one feels like doing. Usually this behavior is grossly exaggerated as it is in overcompensation. Many crusaders probably fit into this category. If one has ever listened to a reformed alcoholic talk, he will know what the above statement means.

Carry Nation, the temperance reformer, must have had a strong unconscious urge to get drunk! Her behavior allowed her not only a release from her urge to drink, but it also served to release much aggression. She did not stop when the whiskey bottles were broken; she wrecked the entire saloon. What wonderful release that must have been! What about the *Elmer Gantry* type preachers? Can they preach against our sins so well because they so intimately know what the sins of man are? What about the old maid who looks under her bed every night? Is she hoping?

To show one example of how defense mechanisms can grow into a full-blown neurosis, a look at the dynamics of *agoraphobia* (a morbid fear of being in an open space) might be helpful. Let's suppose a woman had an overdeveloped conscience with regard to her sexual impulses. These id impulses would be continually trying to come to the surface but her conscience would not let them. The traditional battle between the id and superego would be under way. If this battle became severe enough, or were prolonged over a long period of time, we should expect some defense mechanism to come into play. Projection would be a natural for this situation. "I want sex" would become "They want sex with me." This woman could then develop a reaction formation. She would be very prudish and puritanical. Any mention of sex would offend her. She would probably be ever on the watch for dirty books or magazines. She might even start a censorship crusade. But all of this might still be too close to the original cause of tension, her sexual impulses. All of the things she did would help to remind her that sex is a problem. If this tension continued, what then? Why not a defense mechanism that totally removes her from any reminder that there has ever been any sex in the whole wide world? What about a fear of going outside? It she stays in the house all of the time, no one can molest her. At last, she is safe from her own hidden desires.

Many latent homosexuals employ reaction formation as well as projection. When this mechanism is employed, exaggerated male behavior is apparent. The man likes to hunt, to fish, to tinker around with automobiles, to play poker with the boys, to drink beer, and to chase women. Any activity that is considered the least bit feminine is avoided. This type of man is called a man's man. Why? One woman cannot sexually satisfy this individual because his male ego is so sensitive that he needs constant reassurance. If he does marry, he cannot remain faithful to his wife because of his unconscious tensions.

Regression (retrogression)

This is returning to an earlier stage of psychological development. Rarely, if ever, does a person grow constantly toward psychological maturity. He moves forward, regresses, then moves forward again. Some regression is to be expected in every human being, but severe regression is dangerous. In fact, many psychologists see this mechanism as one of the major underlying explanations for schizophrenia.

Many of the patients in every mental hospital have regressed right out of the real world into a fantasy world. Their actions are childlike in quality and they live in the make-believe world that is so frequently seen during childhood. However, there is a large difference between the fantasy life of a normal child and that of a schizophrenic. The child is able to distinguish between the real world and the make-believe world; the schizophrenic is not.

When the world is full of problems, tension, and pain it is only natural that we may wish to return to an earlier, happier period in our life. One way we can do this is to associate something with that happy period. For example, sometimes a song pops into our mind. We go around all day humming, singing, or whistling this tune. We feel better without knowing exactly why. What has happened is that some of the old feeling has been brought into the present via the association. Our mental regression has helped alleviate some of the present discomfort. Although the above example is not a neurotic obsession, it is an obsession-like tendency. Certainly the real world is not totally full of pleasure. All of us should be allowed some regressions. To act temporarily like a child may have great therapeutic value. It may release many pent-up emotions. The danger comes when a person regresses and remains at this earlier stage of development.

Experimental neurosis has been produced in all sorts of animals in the laboratory. These experiments usually involve forcing an animal to make discriminations which are beyond his capability. For example, a mouse may be rewarded for jumping into a circle but punished for jumping into a square. The mouse will eventually learn to discriminate between a square and a circle. Then if we gradually move the two stimuli closer and closer together, in shape but not in distance, at some point the animal will no longer be able to discriminate between the two forms. When this point is reached, the mouse will develop an experimental neurosis.

This type of neurotic behavior resembles regression very closely. The animal may defecate or urinate indiscriminately. He may become aggressive in a very undirected manner (similar to the undirected rage of an infant when he is confined). In all actions, the mouse will show disorganization, or behavior which we associate with immaturity in humans.

One investigator extended discrimination experiments beyond the usual limits. Masserman (1961) produced experimental neurosis in several cats. Throughout the experiment, two bowls of milk were placed before the cats—one plain milk, the other with a ten percent alcohol content. Before the experimental neurosis occurred, no cat chose the alcoholic milk. After the neurosis, every cat chose this milk. Alcoholic cats were literally produced in a laboratory. Can we generalize from this experiment to human behavior? Is it possible that alcoholism is, at least partly, regressive in nature? Isn't disorganization one characteristic of both alcoholics and schizophrenics?

Fixation

In regression, a person has to develop to a certain point and then return to an earlier stage, whereas in fixation he never progresses beyond a certain stage in various areas of psychological development. Fixation is defined as a stoppage in psychological growth caused by an overinvestment of psychic energy in an object, person, or situation. For example, if a man invests too much energy in his mother, we usually refer to him as a "mama's boy," and we think of him as being psychologically immature. Freudian psychologists see cigarette smoking as a socially condoned substitute for thumb sucking, and once more, the implication is one of immaturity.

Freud thought fixations grow out of too much frustration or too much gratification. It is perfectly normal to invest some psychic energy *(libido)* in other people, objects, or parts of our own body, a process called *ca-*

thexis; but an overinvestment (fixation) causes the individual trouble.

Freud's entire system of psychosexual development grew out of this conceptualization. Thus, if an anal expulsive personality type marries an anal retentive type, the couple will have continuous trouble in their marriage. The first will be generous, love to spend money, and keep the house in a sloppy, disarranged state. The other will be orderly and neat, miserly, and dependable. Their tastes in art will differ because the former will like "smear" art and the latter will like "neat" art. One loves to give, the other loves to save. If children who are messy bother one parent, the other will say, "Why don't you leave them alone?—they are not hurting anything." Their life together will be miserable because one fixated at one period in life and the other fixated at a different period. Their unconscious models, or prototypes, are different. For happiness, the anal expulsive type who loves to give should marry the oral incorporative type who loves to receive (take in).

Whether Freud's conceptualizations with regard to oral and anal fixations are extremely valuable in the understanding of human behavior is debatable. Nevertheless, it does seem that parents can make feeding and toilet training too rewarding or too frustrating.

There are many compulsive eaters, drinkers, and smokers in America. In fact the lips seem to be an important part of our society. Gum chewing, kissing, and sexual activities involving the mouth are popular behavior patterns.

Much can be said with regard to the American attitude toward the elimination of wastes from the body. Some of our favorite slang expressions refer to this process. The relationship between feces and dirt is quite apparent in the middle class obsession with cleanliness. Hand-washing compulsions are not as rare as commonly supposed.

Nomadism

Several types of reactions are defense mechanisms if used occasionally, but if used as a primary adjustment pattern border on a full-blown neurosis. One of these dynamisms is called nomadism. This reaction is characterized by wandering from place to place, job to job, even wife to wife. The nomad stays in a place or a situation for a brief period; tension begins to mount, interpersonal relationships become hampered, and soon the problems are too many and too frequent.

This type of person deals with these problems by fleeing the scene. He tries to run away from the tension, but it never works, largely because the anxiety and tension are internal. He takes his problems with him and in a very short time he is right back where he started. If someone or something stops the nomad from running, a more severe reaction is likely to occur.

Nomadism is illustrated by the following case:

Joe was a young man who had been a nomad since he was thirteen. All of his life he had been running. As a child he constantly ran away from a drunken father. He was forced to run and hide until his father was sober, or be severely beaten. At fourteen he ran away from home permanently. He worked in a circus, followed the wheat harvest, became a traveling musician, drove trucks, and worked on pipelines.

When he was twenty-three, a friend offered to lend him money to go to college. He started college and did quite well for a few months. Then the tension started to mount. He started seeing a girl almost every night. She loved him, but he could not let himself become too involved with her. The pressure increased.

One night he was sitting in the back seat of his roommate's

car on a double date talking to his girl friend. She said something; he lost control of his emotions, and slapped her. To him that was an unforgivable sin because of what he had seen his father do so many times to his mother. All of the tension, pressure, and guilt hit him at one time. He froze into a catatonic stupor (see catatonic schizophrenia). He responded to nothing in his environment. He had to be bodily carried to the hospital.

The psychologist employed a technique similar to hypnotic suggestion in bringing Joe out of the catatonia. Over and over the sentences, "He is going to be all right. He is going to come out of it," were uttered. In a few hours Joe began to relax; the frozen muscles started to thaw. In another hour, Joe was up and around, talking to everyone as though nothing had happened.

An appointment was made for the next day to discuss what had happened. Joe kept this appointment and the story unfolded of the drunken father and submissive mother. This appointment was the last one to be kept. A week later Joe was driving a truck again. He had taken off for parts unknown.

Daydreaming (fantasy; autistic thinking)

Daydreaming is another defensive reaction to anxiety. Everyone daydreams at times and the content of these dreams is surprisingly similar in most people. Most daydreams have to do with achievement, success, money, sex, and security. Daydreaming is one of the easiest of all ways to escape the pressures of everyday living. Whereas the nomad withdraws physically, the daydreamer withdraws psychologically.

Since everyone daydreams at times, it follows that this activity in and of itself is not abnormal. The severity depends upon the degree. When anxiety grows to the point that a person spends much of his time in fantasy thinking, but still is in touch with what is happening around him, he is employing a defense mechanism. When he totally withdraws into a dream world, he is labeled a psychotic. In psychotic withdrawal the person is no longer in touch with the real world. He may sit and stare into space; he may develop catatonic symptoms; he may laugh or giggle at the things the "voices are saying"; he may become belligerent; or he may talk to God. Whatever he does, he withdraws from the real world, a world full of anxiety, tension, conflict, and frustration. Some psychologists assume that this reaction is the last line of defense. If it fails, death will probably ensue.

There are two basic types of daydreams, the *conquering hero* and the *suffering hero*. In the conquering hero type the individual perceives himself as omnipotent, omniscient, and omnipresent. He is all powerful, all knowing, and present everywhere at the same time. He can do anything he wishes, because that is exactly what he is doing — wishing. He can be the greatest writer, poet, artist, musician, scholar, executive, lover, warrior, or athlete in the world. He can be the biggest, strongest, swiftest, and best coordinated man on campus — or in the entire country. He can be wealthy, suave, and sophisticated. His intellect and good looks can make him most attractive to the opposite sex. These grandiose dreams can make failure seem insignificant, push poverty into the background, eliminate competitors, and rid the world of tension, pressure, and problems. If the person starts to believe in the reality of these visions, the system can snowball into a paranoid delusion of grandeur.

In the second type of daydream, or the suffering hero type, the person feels he has been wronged, hurt, or persecuted. Frequently his thoughts drift from the real or imagined injury to retribution and revenge. For example, a young man and his girl friend break up. He may sit in class, daydreaming about the great injustice of it all. At first he may think of ways he can get even. Should he spread some gossip about the girl? Should he try to go out with her best friend or sister?

Then his thoughts may drift to himself. He may become self-critical, self-depreciating, and guilty. Back and forth the thoughts go. What does he do now? What about all the time that has been lost? If his thoughts become more and more depressive, he may consider suicide; he may want to become the absolute suffering hero; he will die of a broken heart. He is too big, too good, too courageous to become vindictive. He will "take it like a man." If these thoughts become too exaggerated or if they are prolonged, they may form the core of an obsession, a compulsion, a phobia, or paranoia.

Free-floating anxiety

This can be a neurotic reaction, but it does not have to be. When this feeling is used as a defense mechanism it takes the form of a general uneasiness or apprehension. We feel tense and anxious. We know that something is wrong, but we don't know what. Many people experience this generalized anxiety the morning after a night of drinking. In fact, this reaction is common when someone has done something that his conscience says is wrong. The anxiety is a moral anxiety that is generalized.

Since unpleasant emotional upheaval accompanies anxiety, it is unlikely that free-floating anxiety will remain in an individual indefinitely. Instead, other defense mechanisms or even more severe reactions are likely to occur. These reactions help to ward off the anxiety but usually complicate the person's life even further.

Free-floating hostility

This is another defensive reaction. If a person perceives the world as hostile he can react to it in kind. The idea seems to be that the best defense is an offense. Attack before you are attacked. Therefore, the person is continually belligerent, hostile, and aggressive. His wit is sharp and cutting. His words drip with sarcasm. If he is a teacher or in some other position of leadership, he becomes a rigid authoritarian. No back talk is allowed. If someone manages to threaten the authority of this individual, he turns on the threatener with the viciousness and predatoriness of a starved tiger. He accuses others of being stupid, lazy, hostile, delinquent, or criminal.

People who live in large cities frequently adopt this manner of dealing with life. Their lives are so hurried and hectic that they have no use for others. If you ask them for change for a dollar, they may answer, "This is what I got up at six o'clock in the morning for? To give you change for a dollar?" Needless to say, when a person meets this type of hostility day in and day out, he can easily become hostile himself. The aggression may become mostly verbal or mostly physical or any combination of the two.

2
neurotic reactions

If defense mechanisms do not serve their purpose of protecting or enhancing the ego, far more severe forms of misbehavior are likely to develop. The second line of psychological defense is the neurosis or psychoneurosis. The neurotic is normal in most respects but shows grossly exaggerated behavior of a specific type. He is in touch with reality but he cannot be considered totally adjusted because his extreme behavior usually alienates him from other people. The neurosis serves to reduce anxiety in the individual but at the same time usually irritates those people around him. Thus, another vicious circle is established.

A person becomes sick to excuse failure, irresponsibility, or irritability. The illness serves to reduce the anxiety within the person and also has secondary reward value in gaining sympathy, attention, and affection. However, after a while associates grow tired of hearing the neurotic complain, rationalize, and project. Their patience and tolerance wear thin. Friction begins to develop. The neurotic is faced with more problems because he has an exceptionally strong need for others. His only out is to go deeper and deeper into his neurosis.

Neurotics are usually egocentric, selfish people on the one side, but they have strong dependency needs and basic insecurity on the other side. They need affection but don't know how to return it. They depend on others but resent their dependency. They realize their imperfection but demand perfection in others. In general, the old adage of being unable to live with people or without people is most appropriate for the neurotic. His need satisfaction is almost totally dependent on others but he constantly antagonizes the very people who can satisfy his psychosocial needs. He cannot live with himself and makes it impossible for others to live with him.

Conversion reactions

The first neurotic reactions to be discussed will be the conversion reactions, which have one thing in common. In all types, psychological anxiety is converted to a physical reaction. Health or concern for health becomes a way of avoiding conflict, frustration, or anxiety. In a sense, all conversion reactions are exaggerated rationalizations. Health provides a suitable excuse for anything.

Hypochondria is a syndrome characterized by unusual concern or preoccupation with health or bodily processes. The hypochondriac is an avid reader of medical literature and, currently, *Reader's Digest* (the medical articles). He indulges in self-diagnosis and self-treatment. He visits physicians constantly and is not satisfied unless he can bring home a new prescription after each visit. When he goes away from home, he takes an extra suitcase to carry the pills. The prescriptions are usually placebos and all of the jars contain approximately the same compound, sugar.

The hypochondriac cannot talk more than five minutes without mentioning his ailments. If needed, he can develop a new set of symptoms every week.

"TV-medicoitis" is a new form of hypochrondria. In this type, a person sees one of the doctor shows on television, develops the same syndrome as the actor patient, and then demands that his doctor treat him in in the same way the the doctor treated his patient on television. If the real physician refuses to behave in the same manner as the TV doctor, the neurotic questions his competence.

Neurasthenia (or asthenic reaction) is a second form of conversion reaction. In this pattern, the physical symptoms are vague. The person describes himself as tired, run down, and worn-out. He has ill-defined ailments such as a nagging backache or ringing ears. The person does not feel good but he cannot tell you what is wrong with him. His back hurts but the pain is not localized.

Neurasthenia is sometimes called the housewife's disease because of its prevalence in this group. The underlying causes are boredom and worry. Probably no work on earth is more boring, routine, and thankless than keeping house. The routine is one continuous process of clean-up, pick-up, and watch-things-get-messed-up-again. The mother is a frequent victim. Everyone in the family takes her for granted. Comments are made only when things are disorderly, never when the house is clean.

In neurasthenia, sleep becomes a way of avoiding the problems of living. However, the process is circular; the more sleep one gets, the more he wants. He begins to feel tired and run down all of the time, no matter how much sleep and rest he has had. Once neurasthenia starts, it is almost impossible to break the pattern. The time to combat this neurosis is before it starts, while one is young. A wide range of interests not only correlates positively with success, but also prevents the appearance of the neurotic asthenic syndrome. Young people who have to be entertained and who can find nothing to do are well on their way to more severe psychological problems in the future.

College students so frequently develop neurasthenic symptoms that the present author calls this reaction the college students' syndrome. It is no wonder that this reaction is so common because college is frustrating and college life is full of problems. Not only is sleep a safe way to get away from these problems; it is also cheap. And most college students have little money for other more expensive escapes. Perhaps, the real wonder is that so few students find this simple and convenient withdrawal mechanism. Very few people get hurt or hurt others while they are asleep.

Hysteria, literally translated means "floating womb." This conversion reaction has the longest history of all the functional disorders. Hippocrates, the father of medicine, named and described it about 2500 years ago. The great physician thought that only women developed these symptoms, thus the name hysteria. Hippocrates recommended marriage as the cure because he thought this would settle the "floating womb." The modern approach to the dynamics of the reaction is not too far removed from the suggestions of the famous Greek. An overdeveloped conscience, especially in regard to sex and aggression, is thought to be the principal contributing factor in all neuroses, including hysteria.

Hysteria is characterized by the appearance of physical symptoms with no known organic cause. The reaction can duplicate almost any organic disease. Hysterical visceral symptoms corresponding to anesthesia, blindness, deafness, paralysis, and asthma have been observed. In most cases, organic diseases have a slightly different pattern so that hysterical symptoms can be detected. For example, one type of hysteria is glove or stocking anesthesia in which a person loses all feeling in an area of the hand and arm or leg and foot resembling the area covered by a glove or a sock. There is a distinct dividing line above which the person can feel, but below which there is no tactile sensation. Organically, this reaction is impossible because physiological anesthesia would correspond to the muscular system and the neural pathways.

Catalepsy is hysterical death. A naive observer would judge a cataleptic to be dead because the reaction is a pathological condition marked by suspension of sensation, muscular rigidity, fixity of posture, and loss of contact with the environment. Throughout the history of mankind, how many of those who have been buried alive or who arose from the dead were cataleptics?

Pseudocyesis (false pregnancy) is hysterical pregnancy. It is possible for a woman to want children so much that she goes through the entire pregnancy sequence from morning sickness to labor. But when labor occurs, there is no baby. How many miscarriages are really false pregnancies in which the physician does not have the heart to tell his patient that she has wished herself into pregnancy?

Hysteria of all types is less common today than it once was. Educated persons are more likely to develop other symptoms, such as hypochondria and neurasthenia. At the present time, the largest incidence of hysteria is among the uneducated or the young. This helps to explain why most of the poeple "cured" by faith healers are from the lower socioeconomic ranks. A person with hysterical symptoms can be cured by prayer, but if there is organic involvement, a physician's care is necessary.

Mass hysteria was at one time in history a common phenomenon. Today it is rare. The reaction involves the spreading of hysterical symptoms from one person to another until a large group of people are reacting in much the same manner. For example, one person may develop hysterical convulsions. Another person may begin to contort in the same manner, then another, and another. Soon an entire group of people may be on the floor twisting and jerking convulsively.

The popular usage of the word *hysterical* differs slightly from the psychological definition. The everyday sentence, "She is hysterical," means she has lost control of her emotions.

Freud did most of his early studies on hysterics. The causal link between sex and hysteria is firmly established. This connection probably led to the early (later somewhat revised) overemphasis on sexual causation of neurosis by Freud. In all hysterical reactions, large segments of life are forgotten. It is surprising that these reactions are relatively rare. What easier way could one find to solve problems than to forget about them?

Dissociative Reactions

Dissociative reactions, which include somnambulism, amnesia, fugue, and multiple personality, have one common characteristic: the individual is able to block off some part of his life from consciousness.

Somnambulism (sleepwalking) is not usually classified as a neurosis, but it does indicate tension or pressure. It is thought by most psychologists that if the pressure is increased or if the problems continue, the sleepwalker will develop more severe symptoms. Therefore, most personality inventories include one or more questions about walking in one's sleep. In somnambulism, the person represses episodes in life but the repression is not so great as to brand the individual as neurotic.

Amnesia is a more drastic form of repression. The person is unable to recall large segments of his life, especially information of a personal nature. For example, a person may not remember his name, where he lives, or whether or not he is married, but he may recall skills quite well. He forgets anything that centers on his problems.

The fugue state is amnesia accompanied by wandering. Not only does the individual forget personal information, he also wanders off in a confused state. Frequently these individuals begin an entirely new life with no memory for their past life whatsoever, as in this case:

> George T., age 35, an auto mechanic, on several occasions found himself in a motion picture theater after having left home to report for work. He would "come to" in a bewildered fashion and would go to a bar for a few drinks. Eventually he would go home.
>
> As a child, George had a pattern of wandering away from home. He came from a very unhappy family; his parents were divorced, and he was left at home with housekeepers. His father was very harsh with him and on several occasions gave him such severe whippings that the neighbors called the police. His mother was a highly emotional person and tried to discipline George by screaming at him and threatening to place him in a boarding home.
>
> In adolescence, he twice found himself going off to school and eventually, "coming to" in a park about two miles from home. In school, George got along well with the teachers and other students. He was a poor student and failed both the second and seventh grades. He quit school at 16 and went to trade school to become an auto mechanic.
>
> George had been married and divorced twice. His first marriage at 19 lasted less than a year because of sexual prob-

lems. He married again at 28 and was divorced three years later because of financial problems. Since that time he has been living alone. He has no children. (Louis P. Thorpe, Barney Katz, and Robert T. Lewis, *The Psychology of Abnormal Behavior—A Dynamic Approach,* 2nd ed. New York: Ronald Press Co., 1961, pp. 226-7.)

When someone tries to fake mental illness, he is likely to feign forgetfullness. Yet, malingering can usually be detected by a trained psychologist. Sooner or later the liar will trip himself up, whereas the amnesiac or the person in a fugue state cannot be trapped because he has forgotten.

Multiple personalities are sensational but extremely rare. This reaction is frequently called "split personality" in popular literature and everyday speech but this is an incorrect term. The multiple personality is characterized by the emergence of two or more distinct personality patterns in a single individual. Quite often, one personality is id dominated (pleasure loving and antisocial) and the other personality is superego dominated (rigid, inflexible, conscientious, and puritanical).

Usually, one personality has no knowledge of the other personality, although this is not always true. In the play, *Three Faces of Eve* (Thigpen and Cleckley, 1957), Eve Black knew about Eve White, but the opposite was not true. Eve White completely repressed the id-dominated Eve Black. This syndrome is the most severe of the dissociative reactions. Not only does the person show extreme repression, he shows almost psychotic withdrawal from reality at times.

Psychasthenic reactions

Psychasthenia is defined as a morbid mental state characterized by mental fatigue, obsessive anxiety,

phobias, and tics. There are several types of psychasthenic reactions. The most common is the obsessive-
compulsive neurosis. This term is linked with a hyphen
because obsessions and compulsions usually occur together, though they do not have to.

Obsessions are irrational, recurring ideas. They may
be called preoccupations but they are usually more persistent and irritating than simple, engrossed thought. An
example of a non-neurotic obsession is the sudden spring-
ing into mind of a tune. One goes around all day humming, whistling, and thinking about this melody. Frequently, this tune comes from a happier period in the
person's life and often it is of a nonsense variety or it is
a singing commercial. The tune lingers on and on, no
matter how hard one tries to rid himself of it.

At the neurotic level the obsession is even more per-
severing and annoying. These thoughts are frequently of
a morbid nature. Death, suicide, or sexual deviation,
perversion, or indiscretion are the types of preoccupations that are often mentioned by neurotic obsessive-
compulsives. The person sometimes becomes so upset
by these ideas that he tries almost anything to shake
them. He may turn to alcohol to deaden his senses, or
he may try to commit suicide. His life is miserable and
he stays in a constant state of agitation unless he can
find a way to rid himself of the enduring, morbid thoughts.
One way he can shake an obsession is to develop a compulsion.

Compulsions are characterized by irrational, recurring
actions. Sometimes the anxiety attached to the obsession
can be discharged by performing some sort of ritual. For
example, the hand-washing compulsion is probably less
threatening than obsessive ideas of guilt. One can wash
away his sins fifty to a hundred times a day.

It is easy to see that in this example, undoing and suppression techniques are combined with the psychasthenia to ward off anxiety in the individual. Other compulsions, such as crossing oneself, picking oneself, or compulsive orderliness are probably as symbolic and more than likely serve the purpose of ridding the person of "vulgar," obsessive thoughts.

Obsessive-compulsive behavior seems to be encouraged by the educational system in the United States. Most graduate students show strong psychasthenic tendencies. They are preoccupied with grades — sometimes even with gaining knowledge. They can be as miserable as the neurotic because if they do try to take a night off, they spend the entire time worrying about what they should be doing. Intellectually they know that everyone needs rest and relaxation, but their personality will not allow them to relax even for a moment. It is for this reason that the obsessive-compulsive reaction has been called the great man's neurosis. Famous figures of the past who were driven to accomplish a specific thing were probably somewhat psychasthenic.

According to the Freudian theory of psychosexual development, the roots of the obsessive-compulsive reaction are in early childhood. The prototype lies in an anal retentive fixation. There is little doubt that American parents are severe in toilet training. This is especially true of middle class parents. Middle class children are most likely to go to college, to become teachers, and in turn, to perpetuate their own psychasthenic approach to life. Middle class Americans are also most frequent travelers to Europe. The first thing they do when they arrive in Europe is to complain about bathing facilities. The "dirty" Europeans are severely reprimanded. Perhaps this explains why Europeans are convinced that all Americans are obsessive-compulsive neurotics.

Skinner (1953) has observed behavior in animals that resembles obsessive-complusive behavior in humans. This pattern has been labeled ritual or superstitious behavior. For example, a pigeon may be in the process of turning as he pecks a key that releases a grain of corn. The turning may become associated with the reward. Later, if one observed this pigeon turning around every time he pecked the key, he could say that this action has no observable value. If he anthropomorphized, he would probably say that he observed an obsessive-compulsive pigeon.

Generalizing to humans, we can speculate that an obsession or a compulsion must have reward value for the individual even though we cannot see the logical connection and even if the individual is not aware of why he does what he does. In fact, most psychasthenics feel that their behavior is silly or futile. Yet they have to go through the ritual or they will break out into an anxiety reaction. Thus, the anxiety-reducing value of an obsession, and more especially of a compulsion, becomes quite obvious.

Compulsive eating, drinking, and smoking are three other common psychasthenic reactions. The chain smoker may be fully aware intellectually that his habit is potentially dangerous to his health. Nevertheless, he has to smoke and he can find all sorts of rationalizations to justify his habit.

The suffix, *mania,* is often attached to a root word to imply a psychasthenic reaction. For example, compulsive drinking of alcoholic beverages is called dipsomania. The dynamics of this and other manias, for example, kleptomania or pyromania, is probably much the same as in the hand-washing compulsion. The object is to escape anxiety. Very few people would question the "escape" value of alcohol.

The attempt to eliminate threat in the environment is easily seen in the person who is compulsive with regard to orderliness. This individual usually has an over-developed conscience. The conscience is continually at war with the id. The tension from this battle is felt by the person but he is not fully aware of why he is so anxious. Therefore, the person becomes afraid but he is not certain why he is afraid.

The tension will continue because this person's conscience will never leave him alone. It is then easy for the fear to be projected onto the entire world. After all, if one cannot trust himself, how can he trust others? Anything different or unusual is to be feared because the delicate balance is upset. This person's entire precarious adjustment depends upon being able to predict exactly what is going to happen.

The way to achieve this predictability is to order life in such a manner that every object and detail fits into a definite pattern. The time schedule must be precise; the sequence of events or thought must be exact; objects must be in place. Nothing must upset the applecart. People who are original, unusual, different, or non-conventional are seen as a direct threat to this neurotic's ego. An attack on his ideas is seen as a personal attack.

Compulsive personalities frequently become authoritarian (Adorno et al, 1950) or prejudiced (Allport, 1958). Since they live in such a threatening world, they tend to distrust the motives of others. The best way to provide a safe and secure world is to dominate others, or if one cannot do this, choose a leader on a white horse, that is, an authoritarian personality who will make others "knuckle under."

Institutions are important because they have a regulating influence on people (and people as individuals cannot be trusted). Conventions are extremely important. Anyone who does not believe in the conventions and mores must be a "red," "nigger lover," "atheist," or "rabble rouser." The labels, or categorizations (Allport, 1958) serve several purposes. First, they help to prevent thinking. If people can be pigeonholed, one no longer has to judge them as individuals, and they can be treated according to the group stereotype. Second, when all opposition is reduced to a single undesirable category, the neurotic can resort to name-calling with all of its emotional connotations. The natural fears in others can be aroused and the name-caller can become a new Messiah, the authoritarian leader of the misguided masses.

Also, categorizations allow a person to project all faults onto the out-group. Nothing is now the fault of the in-group; everything is caused by those outsiders, hippies, or communists. Externalization is the word used by Allport to describe this phenomenon. This mechanism is seen in the fatalistic attitude often shown by prejudiced people; everything depends upon fate. Nothing happens within the individual, therefore, "It was in the stars."

Repression is distinct in this type of individual. His consciousness tells him how nice and loving he is. The corruption and evil in the world, therefore, are the result of others. In other words, the prejudiced personality is so afraid of parts of his own make-up that everyone has to be accused of his faults. If his subconscious is on the verge of chaos, "order" has to be put into it even if you have to beat people into submission.

Superstitions are institutionalized compulsions. For example, in this country one should not cross the path of a black cat, walk under a ladder, or break a mirror. If one brags about himself or his family, he should knock on wood. If he spills salt, he should throw some over his shoulder.

These compulsive patterns are probably conditioned in much the same manner that Skinner conditioned superstitious behavior in his pigeons, although some superstitions may have symbolic value. Knocking on wood may be one of the prehistoric means of getting rid of evil spirits. Black has been traditionally associated with evil and the synonym for cat, pussy, does not have to be given much thought. This superstition expresses quite adequately the American attitude toward sex—It is evil and it should be avoided at all times. The following case illustrates vividly the link between compulsions and sex, sin, and filth:

This boy's excessive cleanliness first showed itself at the age of thirteen, when it was noticed that he washed his hands many times during the day. Later he began to bathe frequently. Frequently he stayed two or three hours in the bathtub. On a number of occasions he daubed iodine on his hands and face. He told his parents that he had scratched himself and wanted to prevent infection. In addition to iodine, he had bought mercurochrome and other antiseptics for use in "emergencies." He also used a boric acid solution to wash his eyes every evening. The parents stated that he refused to play ordinary games with other children because he did not want to soil his hands.

When asked to explain his concern regarding cleanliness, he stated that he realized that he washed more than other boys, but that in his case there were real reasons. He believed that his skin was of such a texture that it retained dirt and germs, and he therefore was forced to wash and scrub himself.

No amount of persuasion was successful in deterring the boy from this until his original conflicts began to be solved. He stated that he had been greatly worried about his guilt regarding his previous activities with other boys. His parents discovered that he took part in sex play and punished him. They had frequently lectured him on the evils of "immoral" behavior and on one occasion, when he was nine, made him sign a pledge never to smoke or drink even beer. They also told how some terrible diseases result from masturbation . . . . He stated that he had "sworn off" masturbating on many occasions, and after each time he masturbated he felt thoroughly ashamed of himself. He also believed that he was deficient in character and will-power because he could not stop. He stated, "I know it's a dirty habit and if anyone finds me out they will think terrible things about me."

After many interviews and much discussion, he began to change his attitude regarding the immorality of his past behavior and the possible consequences of his supposed moral transgressions. His excessive cleanliness gradually decreased and he was able to take part in the activities of other boys without feelings of unpleasantness from soiling his hands and clothes. (M. Sherman, *Mental Conflicts and Personality*. London: Longmans, Green & Co., 1961, p. 169.)

Phobias are classified as a psychasthenic reaction because in a real sense they are obsessive—compulsive in character. A phobia is an irrational, morbid fear which is out of proportion to the danger. Phobias can also be excessive dislikes or distastes. Thus, a person may have a morbid fear of snakes or he may have an obsessive dislike for worms.

At one time it was fashionable to label phobias according to what the person feared; however, since an irrational fear may become attached to any object, person, or situation, the list of phobias became unreasonable. The current trend is to call all phobias the same reaction and deal with all of them in the same manner. The following examples are chosen only as a representative sample:

> Acrophobia—high places (self-destruction)
> Agoraphobia—open space (sex)
> Claustrophobia—closed space (the womb)
> Hydrophobia—water (pregnancy)
> Gynephobia—women (sex)

It is possible that a phobia can be conditioned, that is, learned. A situation may be associated with pain often enough or the pain may be severe enough that the person learns an irrational fear of that situation. For example, a mountain climber may fall several times and ultimately develop acrophobia.

On the other hand, many phobias seem to have symbolic value. The words enclosed in parentheses in the above examples are the Freudian interpretations of what the person is really afraid of. To follow through, on the above example of acrophobia, if one asks a person with this symptom why he is afraid, his usual answer is, "I am afraid I will jump," not, "I am afraid I will fall." The conclusion logically follows that the person has strong conscious or unconscious self-destructive tendencies. He must really be afraid of himself, or at least part of himself.

Mothers teach their daughters to fear snakes, mice, worms, insects, and rats. In Freudian psychology, all of these animals are phallic symbols and, once more, the American woman's attitude toward sex is probably symbolically passed on from generation to generation. Certainly these phobias are out of proportion to the danger and the same can be said of the typical American woman's fear of sex. It was no accident that the serpent was the symbol of sin in the Bible.

The following case is a good example of how a phobia can be conditioned and at the same time symbolic.

Case Study: Anthropophobia. Edna, age 20, sophomore in college.

Chief Complaint: Pronounced fear of being left alone with a man, whether fellow student, professor, relative, or acquaintance. Has refused all dates and never allows herself to be placed in situations where it is necessary for her to go home with someone of the opposite sex. Could give no good reason for this fear, but recognized maladjustment; yet, there seemed to be nothing that she could do about it. Recently when it appeared inevitable that she must go home from a party with a boy, she trembled, her hands became clammy, and she became very faint. As a result her hostess invited her to remain for the night.

Family History: Father died when the patient was 5. Mother remarried when she was 7. Patient and stepfather did not get along well. Mother emotional, frequent temper tantrums. Emotional scene about once a week. No siblings.

Personal History: Edna, according to mother, was father's favorite. When father died, Edna was greatly upset. For almost a week after his death she kept crying for her "daddy." Edna never did get along with stepfather, was frequently punished by him, and came to dislike him intensely.

Began school at 6, has always done well in studies. Very well liked by schoolmates and teachers. Graduated from high school with honors at 18. At present is majoring in education in one of leading universities in the West.

Early childhood history marked by severe traumatic experience that appears to be related to present condition. One evening when she was 8, was left at home alone with male boarder. While parents were away boarder attempted to molest her. Although he did not succeed in gaining his objective, he threatened the child with bodily harm if she ever told anyone about his advances. This she refrained from doing for a number of years.

Treatment: Interview therapy initiated and continued for four months. First few interviews very informal and impersonal. After rapport had been established between patient and therapist, personal and unpleasant episodes in patient's life were dwelt upon. She was finally led to tell story of unwelcome advances of boarder in her childhood. In relating episode Edna became very emotional, wept copiously. Was encouraged to relate the incident over a number of times, each time being reassured that there was nothing shameful about it and that no harm would befall her as a result. Was enabled to understand psychodynamics of phobias in general and of her case in particular. Shortly after first telling of traumatic experience she began to improve. After four-month period of interview therapy had overcome fear to the point where she made first date with one of her classmates. They went to the theater together. (Louis P. Thorpe, Barney Katz, and Robert T. Lewis, *The Psychology of Abnormal Behavior—A Dynamic Approach,* 2nd ed. New York: Ronald Press Co., 1961, pp. 270-1.)

Psychosomatic Reactions

In hysterical reactions, physical symptoms appear with no underlying organic cause. This is not true in psychosomatic reactions. Although the problems or stress may be predominately psychological, the person does ultimately develop actual organic symptoms. For example, the ulcer, which is cited as the classic psychosomatic reaction, is real. There is organic damage and treatment includes physical and psychological therapy.

Hans Selye (1956) has provided the most adequate theory to explain psychosomatic disorders. This theory, called the general adaptation syndrome, consists of three stages: alarm, resistance, and recovery or death.

According to Selye, when the body is subjected to stress, psychological or organic, it becomes alarmed. The body goes into operation to fight the stress, but it can fight in only one way. This reaction is exceptionally complex, but it is always in the same direction. The body is unable to distinguish between various types of stress. Thus, the body only recognizes a general tension level, not whether the stress is psychological or biological.

When the body is faced with a stress, the sympathetic division of the autonomic nervous system goes into operation. This, in turn, stimulates the pituitary, or master gland, which then releases its hormone, ACTH (Adreno-cortico-tropic-hormone) into the blood stream. This hormone, in turn, acts upon the adrenal cortex, which releases a multitude of hormones into the blood stream. These hormones are sent all over the body to resist the stress.

However, while the body is resisting one type of stress, resistance to other types of stress is lowered. Thus, when a person is physically ill, he is less able to resist psychological stress, and vice versa. If a person is in a psychologically stressful situation, which is commonly of prolonged duration, he may develop all sorts of organic symptoms. This is the meaning of the word psychosomatic; the mind and the body are not separate, they function together as a dynamic, interrelated system. If one part of the system is disturbed, all other parts try to restore the balance. There is an attempt to return to equilibrium. From this standpoint, statements such as "mind over body" are ridiculous.

If the body is successful in overcoming the stress, the third stage of the general adaptation syndrome is recovery. If the stress is too severe or too prolonged, the body may be unable to win the battle and the third phase is assumed to be death. Certainly doctors talk about the will to live as a vital ingredient in recovery in cases of severe accident. In the Orient, psychological death is not an unusual occurrence. People decide it is time to die, so they sit down and die. Even in the United States, it is not alarming to hear of one spouse dying a few months after the other one dies, especially when the couple has been married for a long period of time.

Psychosomatic reactions may involve any system of the body or any part of the soma. Some of the better-known psychosomatic conditions are ulcers, migraine headaches, asthma, hives, acne, backaches, bronchitis, and high blood pressure. One author goes so far as to say that the common cold and possibly even some types of cancer are psychosomatic. (Hubbard, 1950). A link between cancer and emotions has recently been established, but the cause-and-effect relationship is far from being determined. No one knows whether the cancer precedes the emotional response, or vice versa.

Psychosomatic conditions have to be treated by physicians because part of the therapy frequently involves the use of medications. It is doubtful though that drugs alone will effectively eliminate the symptoms. Psychotherapy combined with chemotherapy is usually required if the condition is to be permanently cured.

Physicians currently estimate that seventy per cent of the patients they see have psychosomatic involvement or have nothing organically wrong with them.

Many psychosomatic reactions are thought to result from inward-directed aggression. The ulcer victim illustrates the type of problems that lead to a mind-body pathology. Typically, the individual who develops ulcers is a driving, ambitious person on the one side, but an exceptionally dependent person on the other side. The dependency prevents him from expressing anger or aggression when it arises; the ambition causes more situations in which aggression is likely to arise.

When the ulcer-prone person becomes angry, he tends to bottle up his emotions. This bottling up causes internal physiological disturbances which, when prolonged, tend to cause tissue damage. Symbolically, the ulcer victim is being eaten up inside and this is just what happens after a period of time. The dynamics of the migraine headache are very similar. At one time in history, almost all ulcers occurred in men, but today women have caught up. Migraines occur in men and women, but are more common in females.

Hypertension is a condition which, when mentioned in applying for a life insurance policy, will probably preclude insurability. The reason for this is that hypertension is, in one way or another, involved in so many fatalities in the United States. The cause of hypertension is thought to be almost solely psychological in origin. The hypertense patient has almost exactly the same personality formation as the ulcer patient. Following is a description of the pattern according to Coleman:

Person tends to feel continual threat and need to be on guard. Stress may involve chronic hostility and/or anxiety stemming from dependency needs and feelings of insecurity. In many instances appears to result from sustained striving toward high goals with unbalanced life activities that do not permit a "change of pace." Incidence rises rapidly with age, especially between 34 and 64. (Slightly more common among females.) (James C. Coleman, *Abnormal Psychology and Modern Life,* 3rd ed. Chicago: Scott, Foresman & Co., 1964, p. 250.)

3
character disorders

Character disorders is a catch-all classification term that covers a wide variety of symptoms. In general, the common characteristic is that the person's behavior causes him social trouble. Here the similarity among character disorders ends; the category includes behaviors as diverse as enuresis (bed-wetting) and sexual deviations.

Psychopaths

The *psychopathic* (sociopathic) personality is the most outstanding example of a character disorder. Psychopaths are frequently described as people with no conscience, but this is not quite accurate. Everyone has a conscience, though some have stronger inhibitions than do others. Instead of no conscience, the psychopath probably has a weak one or one that is different from the consciences of others.

Psychopaths act out their emotions. If they become angry, they can, and sometimes do, become violent. However, intelligent psychopathic individuals rarely have to resort to violence. They learn quite early in life that flattery is a better approach to getting people to do what they want them to do. Therefore, these people develop a manner that causes others to welcome their company (at least at first). They are masters in the use of flattery, or any other verbal techniques which will accomplish what they want to accomplish.

Because they make others feel so good, they rarely have to resort to more drastic measures to fulfill their philosophy of life, "I want what I want when I want it" — a philosophy involving very little concern or use for other people. They see other humans as objects for exploitation and manipulation. They do not even consider responsibility to others.

On the other hand, some psychopaths show a deep affection for animals. They can become very emotional if they see an animal mistreated. Because they do act out their emotions, they may become extremely aggressive toward anyone they see harming an animal. Herman Goering (Bluemel, 1948) was a criminal psychopath of this type. He did not hesitate to sentence masses of people to death, but showed a great affection for his pets.

One type of sociopath comes from a home in which the mother is almost seductive. This mother fondles her son's genitals (usually under some pretense, such as washing the child or applying medication), forces him to sleep with her until quite late in life, and undresses in front of him. This mother does not realize the seductive aspect of her behavior and would be offended if it was pointed out to her. She refers to the son as "my lover."

When the boy grows up, he has a confused set of values since he was never given a chance to develop his own ego. His mother is included as an integral part of his self-concept. He has little use for humanity and sees people as objects to exploit. However, this type of psychopath has a close attachment to his mother. The slang expression "mother fucker" sends him into a violent rage. The expression itself is too close to the core of his problem (Lindner, 1959).

Many psychopaths come from so-called "good" homes. The father is a successful, respected community leader. The mother is beautiful, sociable, and affable. However, there are other characteristics of the parents that are not readily observed by acquaintances. The father is not only successful, he is also stern, distant, and cold to his children. The mother is not only beautiful, she is also frivolous, shallow, pleasure-loving, and indulgent. Appearances are all-important in this home. Through their actions, the parents show the child that his behavior is not important. What is important is how he appears to others. Thus, the child learns disrespect for the rights of others because, after all, they are so stupid that if he plays his cards right he can get anything he wants from them.

When a person from this type of home becomes antisocial, everyone wonders why. "His home is so good." "He has everything." What people fail to realize is that the appearance of the home is a facade, a false front. Behind the scenes, the parents literally taught the child to be a psychopath, though they are totally unaware of how this happened.

Many children from orphanages become psychopathic in later years. Several studies (Ribble, 1938; Goldfarb, 1956; Harlow, 1960; Spitz, 1965) indicate that when a child (or monkey) does not receive love during early infancy, he may find it extremely difficult to be able to give love in later years. Maternal deprivation has its effect during the first year of life.

Many neglected children develop a condition known as *marasmus* (Ribble, 1938). This syndrome is characterized by physical and emotional wasting away. A large percentage of children who develop this condition die. If the deprivation comes during the second half of the first year, after a good relationship during the first half, the child may develop anaclitic depression or even childhood schizophrenia (Spitz, 1965; Erickson, 1950).

When a child goes into anaclisis, he shows the symptoms of marasmus and withdraws from his environment as well. He loses all interest in the things going on around him and eventually stops responding to the mother or mother substitute. Some children survive this condition to enter adulthood with a condition known as "affect hunger." This condition is characterized by a starvation for affection which is so strong that it is almost impossible for a single person to satisfy it.

In addition, people with affect hunger seem unable to return love even when someone gives generously to them. These unfortunate individuals go through life with almost a single motive, to find love and affection even though they can never find enough and are quite incapable of showing love themselves. Others, who survive maternal deprivation, may live on to become full-blown constitutional psychopaths. If the person lives to age 40, many of the symptoms subside or disappear.

The following case illustrates the charm of a clever psychopath:

Jack——was a 32-year-old male who had been included in Terman's gifted children study. His Stanford-Binet IQ was measured during his childhood to be 168. His mother had died quite early in his life, leaving him and his twin brother in the care of a somewhat antisocial father. The father was a highly successful salesman who loved to go to parties and carouse with women. The twins were left in the care of a baby-sitter, housekeeper, or with relatives most of the time.

At 32, Jack had completed a Master's degree after entering, leaving, and re-entering college several times. He had been married and divorced twice. He had two children by the first marriage and one by the second. He lived in an adjoining state to that of his first wife, and consequently did not pay any child support because the wife would not press the issue to the point of extradition. About twice a year Jack would return home to his first wife, convince her that he was coming back, live with her for two or three weeks as husband and wife, and then leave her again. He was so convincing with his beautiful words and disarming manners that she believed him every time.

Jack married his second wife because she had money and prestige, but he continually ridiculed her "affectation." Finally, after having caught him with several other women, she left him one night after a fight about his carousing. The fight progressed from heated words to physical assault on his part. He struck her a severe blow in the stomach, although she was eight months pregnant. She left him the next day to return to her parents.

After this, Jack obtained a job in a large city as a substitute teacher. Every day, if he worked, he taught whatever subject the schools required. The reports stated that he was excellent in any assignment. During this period he would cruise the bars at night, almost always picking up some woman. He not only obtained sex in this manner, but he succeeded in getting the women to pay all the bills. If he wanted a change of pace, he would telephone a dormitory at a local women's college and talk the girl who answered the phone into going out with him. He practically never failed because he was not only intelligent, quick-witted and charming, but he was also handsome and well-built. He had been a weight lifter for years.

After two years as a substitute teacher, he made the mistake of accepting a full-time teaching job in a junior high school in a small town. He lasted on this job only five months, because one of the many 14-year-olds he seduced informed on him.

Jack returned to the city and lived off women for awhile. During this time he contracted a severe illness. His physician told him that this rare condition was often fatal and that the best he could hope for was the loss of his right leg. He was as blasé about his own impending death as he was indifferent toward the desires, wishes, and motives of others.

The twin brother of Jack— —showed many of the same traits, but he had made a more socially acceptable adjustment by becoming a salesman. The brother bought what he wanted instead of talking people into giving him everything.

Dyssocial personality

There is some similarity between the psychopathic personality and the dyssocial personality. Both can be cold and calculating. Both can turn to a life of crime. Both can and do exploit other people.

But there is one essential difference in the two personality types. The dyssocial person has adjusted to his environment. Within his group, he cannot be called deviant. He has merely learned behavior from a group that is essentially antisocial. For example, if a child grows up in a slum area, he may learn from his peers that it is all right to lie, to steal, to cheat, and to become aggressive against members of the out-group. Girls in this environment may learn that sexually promiscuous behavior is perfectly permissible as long as they receive pay. In some neighborhoods, these attitudes are learned from the parents as well as from neighbors and peers.

When the dyssocial person reaches adulthood, his natural profession is crime. It is as simple as that. He did not become antisocial because of behavior pathology, because his parents were cold and distant, because his mother was overindulgent, or because he came from an orphanage. He is merely doing what he has learned to do, and what he knows how to do best.

It is estimated that about one-third of the people in prison are dyssocial, one-third are antisocial (psychopathic), and the other third are a miscellaneous group of neurotics, alcoholics, psychotics, and sex deviants.

Everyone realizes that crime is big business and that our penal system is a costly institution. Much crime could be stopped if we could clean up our slums, if we could bring poverty under control. The dyssocial person is normal in every respect except one—he learned a value system of a subculture and not of the total society. This problem should be easy to correct. All we have to do is change the models with whom this type of person identifies. Of course, this should be done in early childhood, not after the learned values have become entrenched.

Case Study: Dyssocial Personality.

Thomas B——was referred to the psychologist because of truancy from school and the whopping lies he told when he was in school. He was 12 years old at the time.

During the first interview, Tom told of his love for guns. He stated that he already owned two guns and was saving his money to buy a third, high-powered model. He loved to hunt and roam around in the woods. Some of the animals in the forest were his friends and some were enemies. His favorite friends were the snakes in his swimming hole. They would curl gently around his legs every time he went swimming. His bitter enemy was a wildcat that he had wounded but not killed.

Thomas told of his love for movies, especially gangster and motorcycle gang films. He worked at a poolroom and at the theater cleaning up to earn money to see these movies. He had identified so completely with "Hell's Angels" that he had organized a bicycle gang in his neighborhood and called them "Hell's Devils."

This adolescent boy related with amusement two incidents from his life. The first of these had to do with the time his mother was in a cast from her neck to her hips because of a broken spine. His mother asked his father to roll her over from her stomach to her back. As she rolled over, Thomas and his father had to duck to avoid being shot because she had hidden a shotgun under her, and as she turned, she blasted away at her husband. The second incident was the time the boy's father came home drunk and nude. According to Thomas, his father had walked about a mile home and had strewn his clothes all along the road on the way. When he arrived home, he was completely naked. Thomas thought that both of these situations were funny.

The events leading up to the broken spine in the mother throws some light on some of Thomas's attitudes. The mother had been spotted by a deputy sheriff passed out in the bed of a pickup truck. The law enforcement official had placed her in the back seat of his car and was driving her to jail. Inexplicably, the car door opened and the woman fell out, causing the injury. Mrs. B— —sued the county and collected a comfortable settlement. In fact, this was not her first lawsuit involving injury. She had collected a large sum of money several times over the years in much the same manner.

The shooting incident was also not the first of its kind. Thomas's mother had killed one man, but was freed due to insufficient evidence. She had been in several other shooting scrapes, but fortunately, no one else had been killed.

Thomas was born in wedlock, but he had a younger brother and sister (both of whom were retarded) born after his mother had divorced his father. At the time of the first interview, Thomas was living with his maternal grandmother and his mother was living in another state, getting started on her third marriage. None of her children were with her. Thomas lived in a home including his grandmother, his retarded brother, an uncle fresh out of prison, and an illegitimate cousin. His sister was living at a school for the retarded.

The second encounter with Thomas came a few weeks later. During this interview, he wanted to talk mostly about several older girls that he had persuaded to become "mamas" in his bicycle gang. He described in vivid terms the sexual activities of his friends and their girls. Thomas also stated that his mother was coming home and was going to take him back to live with her. After this, Thomas became totally disinterested in the threats of the truant officer. He knew that he could evade him.

Thomas didn't bother to go back to school. An arrangement was made between the welfare department and the school officials whereby the truancy would be overlooked if the grandmother would bring him in for counseling once a week. Rapport had been established between the boy and the psychologist, so Thomas readily agreed to this condition. On the first visit under this arrangement, the grandmother informed the psychologist that she was to see Judge— —after the interview. The boy and his grandmother were seen together. Mrs. L— —talked openly about how unmanageable Thomas was. She said that he just wouldn't listen to anything she said, so she had given up trying. Thomas smiled and agreed.

A few minutes after this interview was over, the psychologist received an urgent phone call. Mrs. L— —was sobbing and weeping. Thomas was in jail. The courts had not been informed of the arrangement to let him stay out of school. The psychologist and the chief social worker from the welfare department rushed over to the jail and explained the situation to the judge. All through this, Thomas sat in his cell disinterestingly smoking a cigarette. He was released in the custody of his grandmother.

Two weeks later Thomas's mother came to take him back to her new home. But a month after this, the mother and son returned home for a vaction. One morning Mrs. B— —arose before everyone else, packed her suitcases, and left without taking Thomas with her. No further arrangements could be made with the courts. Thomas was sent to training school "for his own good."

Sexual deviation

Contrary to popular opinion, most sexually deviant people are not oversexed; they are undersexed. In fact, most of them have an overdeveloped conscience with regard to sex. Their deviant behavior, in many cases, is simply less threatening than normal sexual relations. Their attitude is immature and naive. Misconceptions and misunderstanding are common. Freud saw sexual deviation as a fixation at the pregenital stage of psychosexual development. The mouth, the anus, and the Oedipus situation do seem to be involved in many so-called abnormal sexual relationships.

As a rule, the sexually deviant individual comes from

a strict, puritanical background. The parents, especially the mother, feel that sex is dirty, vulgar, evil, sinful, and nasty. The child's parents rarely tell him anything other than "Don't do to. It is bad. You'll go to hell if you do." Thus, what the child learns is learned in the streets from peers who are usually as naive as he is.

No area is as emotionally loaded in America as sex. Forty-eight states have laws against normal sexual relations, covered by one or more of the three terms: adultery, fornication, or cohabitation. Rarely are these laws enforced. In fact, if they were, the majority of the adult American population would be behind bars.

The situation is complicated even more in the forty-nine states that have laws against so-called abnormal sexual relations. These sodomy laws rarely spell out what is considered a crime. In fact, the wording is usually so vague and ambiguous that almost any behavior could be considered "a heinous crime against God and nature." As can easily be seen, the emotionality is so evident that one would probably be called a "communist atheist" if he dared speak out against these rather ridiculous infringements of individual rights. Because of the ambiguity of the laws, people can be, and have been, convicted on the basis of circumstantial evidence alone. The prison sentences vary from state to state, but are frequently quite severe on a second conviction. For example, a person can go to prison in North Carolina for sixty years for mouth-genital contact which the Kinsey Report showed more than sixty per cent of all college graduates practice. In Wyoming or Indiana, a person can go to prison for heavy petting.

Of course, everyone knows that people are rarely sentenced for sexual deviation. Nevertheless, the fact that the laws are on the books helps to create an attitude of disrespect for all laws. People seem to feel,

"Laws were made to be broken. Just don't get caught." As long as these laws exist, a sexually deviant person is in a position that unscrupulous people, including law enforcement officers, can take advantage of. The deviant can be blackmailed at the discretion of anyone who knows his secret.

The American attitude toward sex is so inhibited that only one sexual outlet is permitted, and that outlet has to be postponed for years until the person can finish his education and support a family. Marriage is the only approved institution for sexual relationships and many people seem to feel that sex is not even acceptable in this setting unless its purpose is reproduction. These people say, you are an animal if sex becomes something pleasurable. They fail to realize that sex for reproduction alone is inherently more bestial; the lower one goes in the phylogenetic chain, the smaller the incidence of non-procreative sex.

The double standard of teaching about sex in the United States makes an overdeveloped conscience almost inevitable in women. For twenty years, everyone tells a girl "Don't do it." Then one day a short ceremony is performed and the newlyweds are handed a slip of paper. Now, all of a sudden, sex is all right. But for most women the twenty or more years of conditioning have had their effect. For a few months, she can forget her inhibitions and prohibitions, but after a while her conscience wins the battle with the id. She begins to feel dirty, vulgar, evil, or sinful.

Rationalizations begin to be used to avoid sex. These excuses, such as headache, backache, fatigue, and sleepiness, are not only for her husband; they are for her. She feels like a legal prostitute and the feeling is not comfortable. Her conscience has put a wall around her emotions. Sooner or later, it puts a wall between her and her husband because he is unable to stand the constant rejection without building some defenses of his own. It is no wonder that sexual deviation is common in America. The overall approach to sex is so restrictive, inhibitory, and derogatory that almost every American has some sickness in his value system. Sex and sin are so intimately linked together that very few people escape the tyrant conscience that makes eternal hell an ever-present threat.

Impotency is a lowered sexual appetite in males. This term also includes an inability to have sexual relationships. The impotent male is unable to achieve an erection or is plagued with premature ejaculation, or he has little or no interest in copulation. Whatever the symptoms, there are probably few cases in which the impotency is physiological. Impotency is usually in relation to a specific person, rarely to all members of the opposite sex.

If a male has an overdeveloped conscience, he may be unable to have a relationship with a woman he does not love; or even if he does love her, he may require marriage to justify the act. Or in the same vein, a man may have a strong attachment to someone else and thereby become impotent with the present woman.

The problem is complicated even further if alcohol enters the situation. Contrary to popular belief, alcohol is a sexual inhibitor, rather than a stimulant. If a man picks up a woman in a bar or at a party, his drinking could interfere with his performance. If then, as a consequence, he starts to worry about his masculinity, the resulting apprehension can, and sometimes does, inhibit future relations. A vicious circle is set up.

Anxiety probably accounts for most impotency. This fear may be moral, neurotic, or real. For example, if the person fears getting caught, getting trapped, catching veneral disease, or becoming emotionally involved with the other person, the psychological conflict could produce an impotent reaction.

Latent or overt homosexuality can produce an aversion to the opposite sex that is so strong that a male may avoid contact, or if he does have contact, he may be totally unable to follow through on the slight attachment he has formed. If the homosexuality is overt, the person is aware of his problem and usually knows what to do about it. However, if the homosexuality is latent, the person does not know what is wrong. Because he is probably already concerned about his masculinity, any failure with the opposite sex tends to exaggerate his problem and he gets on a merry-go-round that never seems to stop. Many individuals in this situation find alcohol a temporary escape. Alcohol can also serve as a rationalization for them. It justifies their impotency to them and to women.

Frigidity is the female equivalent of impotency. It is probably much more frequent than impotency because of the rigid, inflexible teachings so many women have received with regard to sex. The above mentioned attitudes toward sex, vulgarity, and evil are an integral part of sex instruction for a large percentage of women. In addition, fear of pregnancy, venereal disease, a bad reputation, and the problem of dependency upon men make sex an exceptionally complex psychological situation for women. If the man does not understand the delicacy of the situation, he can easily turn the woman against sex. However, as with impotency, frigidity is probably only rarely physiological. A woman who is frigid with one man may be totally different with another.

The same things that were said about impotency can be said about frigidity. Fear, anxiety, bad teaching, latent and overt homosexuality are probably the major causes. Understanding between the sexes can go a long way in reducing the incidence of both.

Many husbands and wives reach a point in their marriage where one or both become uninterested in sex with their mates. This situation illustrates the psychological complications that can lead to impotency and frigidity. If the woman is inhibited with regard to sex, she will find all sorts of excuses to get out of this unpleasant activity. The man's ego is involved in this situation because he has been taught that sex is a measure of his masculinity. Because of this ego involvement, he reacts emotionally. He may become angry; he may have his feelings hurt; he may pout and sulk. At any rate, both partners begin to exaggerate their real and imagined hurts.

The psychological climate has then reached a point where sexual relations with the spouse are drudgery rather than something pleasurable. Then both partners sometimes begin to feel that there must be somebody else. This may or may not be true, but the person's perceptions are as important as is the reality. As with most other abnormal reactions, a vicious circle is established and things go from bad to worse. In this circle trust has been hampered. Trust along with respect are the cornerstones of a happy, successful marriage. When one or the other, or both, is lacking, marriage is at best mediocre, and at worst a miserable failure.

American women almost universally want a man they can respect. However, they do not want a cave man. The balance between being a leader, a decision maker, someone that can be looked up to and a person who disregards the wishes, desires, attitudes, and needs of the woman is a razor's edge. If a man makes important decisions without consulting his wife he can destroy the feelings she has for him. On the other hand, if he can never make a choice, if he continually lets his wife "wear the pants" in the family, she loses respect for him.

Sex problems become only one of many signs that the couple have not made an adjustment to one another. They usually disagree on almost everything, from child rearing and finances to attitudes toward sex. Psychologically they are incompatible, so it is only natural that they are sexually incompatible. Sex can, and often does, become the whipping boy.

Satyriasis and nymphomania refer to an exaggerated desire for sexual relations; satyriasis being the condition in males, and nymphomania being the female counterpart.

As the suffix *mania* of nymphomania would suggest, the reaction is considered to be of an obsessive-compulsive type. There is a value judgment involved in what is enough and what is too much of anything. Certainly there are wide individual differences in sexual appetite as well as in any other appetite.

If nymphomania (or satyriasis) can be called a deviancy, it has to take on a compulsive character. The person has to be preoccupied with sex. His entire style of life must be centered around sex, sexual thoughts, and sexual conversation. This would imply a defensive system and the person would probably be overcompensating, suppressing, and reacting against something else. This, in turn, would imply that the nymphomaniac or satyr is undersexed. For example, a person may be a latent homosexual and because this is so threatening, he may employ a reaction formation; that is, he may behave just the opposite of the way he feels.

This person would show exaggerated behavior. If male, he would indulge in activities considered all-male, such as hunting, fishing, mechanics, poker playing, beer drinking, and chasing skirts. He would delight in showing his sexual prowess by "conquering" many women. If female, she would show exaggerated feminine behavior. Going to bed with a large number of men serves the purpose of warding off the unconscious threat. It proves to others, as well as to the woman herself, that homosexuality never entered her mind.

Sexual behavior, like alcohol or drugs, can be used to escape from problems. In satyriasis or nymphomania sex is used this way. It takes on an addictive character much the same way that some people can be addicted to bridge, golf, or television. Sex is employed as a suppression technique; the person stays busy to forget. Since sex is so threatening to most Americans, the choice of this behavior as a suppressor usually complicates problems rather than reduces them.

Betty was a young college student with a severe, fundamentalistic religious background. During her first year in college, she met and fell in love with Sam. They dated every night, with increasing physical intimacy which finally ended in sexual intercourse. At first, love justified the act to Betty, but soon her overdeveloped conscience began to create internal conflicts. She wanted to return to the pre-intercourse relationship, but Sam was persistent. He would not allow this, so the couple argued more and more. Eventually, they broke up because neither could understand the other. At that time, Betty's conscience really bothered her.

During this period she got drunk and went to bed with another boy. This eliminated the guilt feelings about Sam, but now her conscience would not leave her alone about the second boy. She used a third to rid herself of guilt over the second. A fourth was required to get over the third.

Soon Betty had quite a reputation on campus. The boys talked about her, tried to date her, and even shouted obscenities at her when she walked past the men's dormitory. Her conscience bothered her more and more. She made resolutions, but they could not be kept because her tyrannical conscience made life so miserable for her that sooner or later she had to escape. She turned to alcohol. She finally had to leave school because her reputation became common knowledge to everyone including the administration. Betty was far from oversexed. In fact, she was just the opposite. Her strict religious upbringing drove her to desperate, exaggerated behavior.

Promiscuity and prostitution, indiscrimate sexual behavior and sex for pay, are probably closely related. Since the labels are rarely attached to men, the discussion of both centers around women and the dynamics are very similar to that of nymphomania. Most promiscuous girls or professional prostitutes are man-haters. Frequently, their history includes a father who left them or a father who was cruel. Their behavior is a symbol for belittling men. If the man is forced to pay for something as natural as sex, he must indeed be little. Underlying this attitude toward men is often a strong personality with a desire to compete with men on their own terms. Men are to be reduced at any price, and sex becomes a useful tool for this purpose.

Many prostitutes allow their latent homosexuality to come to the surface. They have girl friends who provide them with the only satisfactory sexual experience they have. Relationships with the opposite sex are neutral or, at times, even repulsive. Another indication of the man-hater complex is the tendency of many prostitutes to have a "kept man." This man is often effeminate, submissive, and homosexual. He has no sexual relations with his mistress. His function is to show off the lavish gifts his mistress has given him. In others words, he is a symbol, a symbol of the affluence of his mistress plus a symbol of the superiority of women.

Disturbed family relationships are usually found in cases of promiscuity and prostitution. As already mentioned, some of these women come from broken homes. An especially common pattern is one in which the father deserts the family and the mother develops a man-hater attitude. When this happens, she can poison her daughter's mind so that she, too, becomes a man-hater.

The daughter strikes out at the world in an area that is sensitive to the puritanical. She reduces men but she also reduces sex to something that has a price tag. Her attitude is frequently cynical; she feels that humanity is rotten and that she might as well join the rat race. As can be easily seen, this attitude could develop in other disturbed family situations, for instance, a rejecting home or a home in which the parents are too strict.

Sexual delinquency is almost always charged against girls. A boy can indulge in the same behavior without being called delinquent. In fact, if sex were omitted from juvenile delinquency charges against girls there would be little delinquency among adolescent girls. However, since sexual promiscuity is considered a crime among girls, it probably requires more emotional disturbance in them than in boys to drive them to this extreme behavior. Studies (Lion et al., 1945) show that most delinquent girls are naive with regard to sex and that the girls are, in general, undersexed. In other words, the general rule with regard to sexual deviancy, that is, lack of knowledge about sex and lowered sexual appetite, seems to apply in some cases of promiscuity and prostitution.

Dyssocial personalities and antisocial personalities can find their way into prostitution. Because of the lucrative nature of the profession, it becomes a natural occupation for women with this type of personality formation. There is little doubt that some girls learn to become prostitutes from their mothers or other people in their immediate environment. To them, prostitution is merely a business that pays well. They live in a microcosmic society rather than the macrocosmic culture.

They would probably have little trouble in a society that condoned prostituion, but because of the illegal nature of the activity in America they can be, and frequently are, exploited. If they have no character malformation when they begin, they will most probably develop one after being in the profession for a period of time simply because of the type of associates they have. Just as other professions, for example, police work, can generate a cynical attitude toward people, prostitution can make one extremely antisocial after a few years in the business.

Rape is one of the most emotional subjects in the United States today. This is shown in the severe laws in most states. Rape is frequently classed with murder and treason and often carries a death penalty (this is especially true if the rapist is a member of a minority group). Just how many of the so-called rape cases are actual rape is hard to determine. Law in the United States is designed to protect women, and a woman can have a man convicted on rather superficial grounds if the emotional atmosphere is charged enough.

Sociologists have recently studied the role of the victim in crimes against persons. They now seem to feel that in many of these crimes, such as murder, assault, and rape, the victim may not be as innocent as was once supposed. Many rapist have been led on by the victim, and then when the victim tries to turn back the clock, it is too late. Many women, consciously or unconsciously, act seductively to a man for various reasons, and when he follows through on their suggested behavior, they are quite surprised and alarmed.

In actual cases of rape, the man involved can usually

be classified as an antisocial personality. More often than not, he has been in other trouble with the law. Many rapists are married men with a family. In a study of married rapists, Palm and Abrahamsen (1954) found a tendency for the wives to be seductive but rejecting. These investigators also found that the mothers of these rapists could be characterized, in general, as the same type of woman.

This probably accounts for the violence so frequently associated with rape. The man is striking out against his mother and wife specifically, but also against women in general. The rapist wants to hurt and he reaches a point where he does not care whom he hurts. Sometimes it is the first woman to come by. Little regard is given to how the woman looks.

Rape victims, in addition to physical injury, often develop psychological reactions so that their relationship with their family is severely damaged. Even if the wife recovers well, the husband may withdraw psychologically, and unconsciously blame his spouse. Marital relationships are especially disturbed when the husband is forced to watch the rape.

When a gang of boys or men rape a single woman, the consequences are especially severe. Almost always, the woman suffers psychological shock that lingers on and on. Some of these women never recover; many have to be institutionalized as schizophrenics. Withdrawal from reality can become the final escape from a harsh, cruel world. However, these cases are probably much less frequent than popular literature would suggest. In fact, psychologists rarely find the single traumatic event to be a cause for mental illness as is so frequently portrayed in novels and movie dramas.

Masturbation is so common that it is doubtful that it can be called abnormal except in a few special cases.

These cases involve masturbation as a distinct preference to the more usual heterosexual outlets or as compulsive behavior with no social restraints.

Sexual restraints are usually one of the first behavior patterns to change when a person develops a psychosis. In mental hospitals, it is not uncommon to see several people engaged in the act of self-stimulation at any time during the day or night. This observed lack of inhibitions among mental patients led many adults of the past to the conclusion that the masturbation caused the mental illness. In fact, everything from weak eyes to a weak mind has been blamed on masturbation.

In the not too distant past, parents and other adults made it a point to frighten the wits out of their sons, and sometimes their daughters, by enumerating the damages they could do to themselves by masturbating. The fear generated by this approach has produced strong emotional conflicts among adolescents for decades.

The adolescent who is unmarried has no socially approved sexual outlet in the United States. Yet he does have biological drive for sex. If he has been conditioned to fear the consequences of self-stimulation, he has conflicting emotions set into motion. For males, interest in sex reaches its peak during the teen years, but a large majority of teen-agers have no approved outlets. This situation leads to an increased possibility of masturbation. If he has been taught to fear this act, he may promise himself that he will not indulge in it.

When the pressures increase, as they almost inevitably do in this society of vicarious stimulation (through movies, pornographic literature, and suggestive ads), he may give in to the least threatening of all sexual outlets, masturbation. Then he becomes afraid that he has injured himself.

This fear leads to a renewed resolution, "I will never

do that again." Over and over, he fails to live up to the expectations of his ego ideal. He is afraid—afraid that he is harming himself physically, that he is going to lose his mind, that he is weak because he cannot control himself. Maybe someone has "lost his mind" because of masturbation. But if anyone has, the cause was the unrealistic fear instilled by his parents or other not-so-well-meaning adults, not the act of masturbation itself.

Since fantasies normally accompany masturbation, it is of much value to try to analyze the content of these visions. These fantasies can be of value in determining whether or not the condition is normal. If there are persistent fantasy thoughts about violence and aggression, one may assume some abnormality. Or one would presume this to be true if the daydream centers around a member of the same sex. On the other hand, if these daydreams are made up of so-called normal content, only some condition of the act itself would label it as normal or abnormal.

It is reasonable to assume that masturbation, under usual circumstances, is normal and that it will not harm one's health. Kinsey et al. (1948 and 1953) reported some incidence of masturbation at one point in the person's life in a majority of males and females, 92 per cent in the former and 62 per cent in the latter group. It is most common among young, unmarried males, especially middle class adolescents who receive a good education. Women are much less likely to indulge in this activity at all socioeconomic and educational levels. Before marriage, girls are more likely to find a sexual outlet in heterosexual petting than they are in masturbation.

If masturbation continues into adult life, it is more likely to be a sign of personality disturbance, especially if the person remains unmarried. Extreme fear of or aversion to the opposite sex could produce this behavior as an enduring sexual substitution. In some instances, a man may be impotent with the opposite sex but quite capable of masturbating, as in the following case:

> William was a thirty-five year old bachelor. His relations with women had always been poor. His mother was elderly when he was born and was a religious fanatic. His older sister (much older) was a driving, ambitious woman who continually competed with the men in her life. In Freudian terms, she was a castrating female who did a very effective job of diminishing her younger brother. When he grew up he had one satisfactory relationship with a woman. This was a married woman of very high intelligence but somewhat lowered moral restraints. She recognized the severe inferiority feelings in William and must have seen him as a challenge. After much coaxing and patience, this woman persuaded him to have a sexual affair with her. Soon after the affair began, she dropped him and left town.
>
> After this affair, he was no longer able to have a relationship with any woman. He started to drink more and more. This was the only way he could get up the nerve to pick up a woman. But, the alcohol combined with his personality made this situation even more complicated. He wanted an affair with a woman to help prove his masculinity, but he did not have the nerve to make a contact with a woman unless he was drinking. And while drinking, he was totally impotent. He began to worry more and more about his impotency. This worry, in turn, increased his desire to drink. All during this period, he was able to masturbate quite satisfactorily. His impotency was only in conjunction with the real thing, a woman. Women had been his downfall; his mother crippled him for life by instilling a fanatic conscience; his sister successfully castrated him by competing with all men, her younger young brother included; his only love affair came about because a woman saw in him a challenge to her feminity. Latent homosexuality produced impotency; impotency produced a desire to drink; and alcohol produced impotency. The vicious circle was in full motion.

Masturbation can be used aggressively. It has been

known that men or boys try to shock or get even with women by masturbating in front of them. Sometimes exhibitionists perform this act in the process of exposing themselves. It is not even unknown for the witness to encourage the act especially in darkened movies or in other situations where the encouragement can remain undetected by others. Voyeurists frequently masturbate while they are peeping.

Mutual masturbation can, and does, occur. This is most likely to occur between members of opposite sexes but has been performed by members of the same sex. In some states, this activity is illegal and is punishable by varying prison sentences. In general, the activity is covered by sodomy laws. In Wyoming and Indiana, heavy petting, or mutual masturbation, carries maximum prison terms of fourteen and ten years respectively.

Incest refers to sexual relations between relatives. Almost every society on earth has a taboo against incest, but the nearness of the family relationship which is prohibited varies considerably from one culture to another. In the United States, the strongest sanctions are against incest among members of the immediate family, namely, between brother and sister, father and daughter, or mother and son. Some eyebrows are raised when first cousins marry, but such marriages do happen without serious legal repercussions.

Incest has been approved, and even considered desirable, by a few cultures throughout history. In ancient Egypt, the most desirable partner for marriage was a brother or a sister. The ruling families of Europe have followed a pattern of close inbreeding. However, most societies have prohibited incest, probably because of the real or imagined dangers of this practice. Undesirable recessive genes are more likely to show up when close relatives marry.

Whatever the reason or reasons, incest among close relatives is taboo in the United States and carries a strong negative emotional connotation. Therefore, the relationship is usually considered a deviancy even though the choice of sex objects is normal in the sense that it is between members of the opposite sex.

Incestuous relationships between brothers and sisters are probably the most common. This is especially true when the brother is the older sibling and the two are required to share the same bedroom as adolescents. Occasionally a father (or more often a stepfather) will force relations on his daughter. These cases can be quite traumatic for the girl, especially if she runs into strong aversions against this type of relationship.

Some teachers, ministers, and well-meaning friends have been known to precipitate the trauma years after the act occurred. The amount of psychological damage that is done probably depends largely on the emotionality of the girl herself, as well as the advice of her acquaintances. If enough damage is done, the girl may go through life as a man-hater or she may even develop homosexual preferences.

In college counseling one hears of forced incestuous relationships not infrequently, but the counselor does not always know whether to believe these stories. Some girls come to counseling with a preconceived notion of what the counselor wants to hear. If their lives do not correspond to what they think he wants to hear, they will make up a suitable story. A wicked stepfather forcing them into a sexual relationship is a beautiful rationalization for anything that may be wrong with them.

Homosexuality refers to a sexual relationship between members of the same sex. Mouth-genital contact is the usual mode of accomplishing this act, but not the only one. *Fellatio* is mouth-genital contact with a penis and *cunnilingus* is the female equivalent. *Pederasty,* or anal intercourse, is another common practice among homo, sexuals. Any one of these three may be found in a heterosexual relationship also.

Contrary to popular opinion, homosexuals are not easily recognized. It is true that some homosexuals advertise their deviation but they are the exception rather than the rule. Most go to great lengths to hide their deviancy because the American attitude toward homosexuality is so derisive. Males will find their way into masculine activities, marry, and have families as a cover-up.

Frequently, they are forced into undesirable activities because they are on the fringe of society. Ridicule, scorn, and even blackmail are employed against them. Therefore, their homosexuality can become a way of life. They have to be preoccupied with their sex life because society forces them to be. They can, and do, lose their jobs, status, families, and reputations if they are caught. Because of this, they frequently become masters of the facade.

Male homosexuals are not all hairdressers, interior decorators, or musicians. They frequently engage in so-called all-male activities, including professional athletics, military service, and weight lifting. These activities have the advantage of close contact with many other males as well as eliminating doubt as to their potential homosexuality. The same applies to lesbians; they are not all physical education majors.

The *Kinsey Report* (1948) indicated that approximately four per cent of the total adult population was solely homosexual, but this probably understates the case. No one really knows how many homosexuals there are in the United States. As civilizations become more advanced, history has shown an increasing incidence of the condition. Greece and Rome became notorious for rampant homosexuality. Some of the most notable figures in history were probably homosexuals, men like Socrates, Alexander the Great, and Leonardo da Vinci.

Actually, what two consenting adults do in private is no concern of anyone else. If the American attitude were more tolerant of homosexuality, the many other abnormalities that usually accompany homosexuality would probably be reduced. However, this is not to say that homosexuality is a superior way of life as many of the verbal deviants are now trying to tell the world. Most homosexuals have behavior pathology other than their sexual deviancy.

In Freudian theory, everyone goes through a homosexual stage of development and, therefore, everyone is a potential deviant. Overt homosexuals usually have an immature outlook and approach to sex. As a rule they have an overdeveloped conscience or a strong fear (or dislike) of the opposite sex. This personality information makes normal sexual relationships difficult or impossible. Therefore, deviant sexual relations become less threatening than normal relations with the opposite sex.

The ranks of homosexuality include people with wide individual differences. Among males, homosexuals vary from men who have identified almost completely with females ("a swish") through men with a fetish (like the "golden stream queen") to complete sadists. The same applies to lesbians, as some of the slang expressions imply; "bull" or "dyke."

In *transvestism* the identification with the opposite sex is so complete that the individual likes to dress in the clothes of the opposite sex. Men will wear makeup, long hair, dresses, stockings, garters, brassieres, and women's jewelry. Women will have their hair cut, wear men's suits, undershorts, and other items of male attire. Some night clubs capitalize on transvestism with their female impersonators. Quite often, there are elements of fetishism in the clothing and objects that the person wears.

Constitutional factors enter into some cases of homosexuality, as in hermaphrodites or in individuals whose hormone balance is severly disturbed. However, environmental factors probably account for the largest percentage of the cases.

As was previously mentioned, everyone goes through a homosexual stage of development. This stage, coming usually between the ages of five and twelve, is characterized by a close affinity to members of the same sex and antagonism for members of the opposite sex. Little boys tend to form gangs excluding girls, though a tomboyish girl may be accepted.

If a homosexual experience happens during this period, it can easily become the preference of the individual. In fact, many people do seem to be started on the road to homosexuality be being seduced by an older homosexual during their earlier, formative years.

Because of the general unhappiness, self-hate, and group hate that homosexuals usually show, it would probably be wise to screen applicants for public school teaching positions for homosexuality. This is not to say that all homosexuals are perverted enough to seduce children. They are not. Most homosexuals have a deep repulsion for any type of child molester, whether a homosexual or a heterosexual.

Fear of the opposite sex accounts for some homosexuality. One way that this fear can develop is to have a feared opposite-sexed parent. For example, if a girl's father is so awesome that she trembles every time she is near him, she could generalize this fear to all men. She may become a lesbian because she can never learn to trust men. Or, as frequently happens when one has a feared parent, identification with the opposite sex may be quite strong because this is one of the best of all ways to reduce a threat—become so much like the threatening object that it is no longer a threat. In this case, the female would identify so closely with the masculine role that she could never have a satisfactory relationship with a man.

If the male-female dominance roles are reversed in a home, the children can learn inappropriate sex roles from their parents. A young man who has learned a feminine sex role may be abused and ridiculed so much by his peers that he joins the ranks of homosexuals because they are the only group that will accept him. The young man in *Tea and Sympathy* could easily have been driven away from normal sexual relations by his classmates. He was fortunate to have an understanding woman on his side.

The same type of trouble can arise when one parent is missing because of death, divorce, or separation. Under normal circumstances more damage is done when the father is missing than when the mother is gone. The reason for this is that mothers more frequently try to take on both jobs, father and mother. If a man's wife is missing, he will usually try to obtain some female help in rearing his children.

Rearing a child as though he were a member of the opposite sex can be quite devastating. If a little boy is made to wear dresses and is kept in curls until he is older, he can learn totally inappropriate behavior directly. These cases are rare but they do happen. Usually the parents themselves are maladjusted and this does not make the situation any easier for the child.

Prisons are breeding grounds for homosexuality and

bisexuality. The estimates of incidence of homosexuality in American prisons generally run around eighty per cent. A young man committed to prison is sought after by the old "wolves." If he refuses the advances of these hardened reprobates, he may be seriously injured or even killed.

Only one state in the United States, Mississippi, has tried to do anything about this deplorable condition. Mississippi allows the wives of married prisoners to visit them on weekends. Where prolonged heterosexual frustration occurs, as in prisons or in the military, homosexuality becomes rampant. Many individuals leave these situations as bisexuals i.e., they will indulge in sexual relationships with men or women, or as confirmed homosexuals.

Latent homosexuality refers to the situation in which a person does not realize his unconscious homosexual tendencies. Overt homosexuals may be unhappy people but are rarely dangerous. On the other hand, the latent homosexual can explode under the right set of circumstances. This is especially true of males.

Since males occupy a favored position in American society, the possibility of homosexual tendencies is quite painful to many men. Rather than admit to themselves or others that this possibility exists, such a man devotes almost all of his energy to covering up, to defending his very delicate male ego.

He spends his time pursuing masculine activities. He likes the things that are labeled as manly; he likes to hunt, to fish, to tinker with machines, to play poker, to drink beer, and to seduce women. The more women he can conquer the better, because this proves his manliness, not only to others but to himself. A wife or girl friend who consciously or inadvertently threatens to bring the homosexuality to the surface by suggesting that he is a poor lover may be violently assaulted. In fact anyone who dares to expose this defect in the person's character can easily find himself the victim of a sudden aggressive outburst.

Latent homosexuals are quick to accuse others of homosexuality. They ridicule and scorn anyone who happens to have the slightest trace of femininity. They delight in organizing "queen hunts" in which a homosexual is picked up, led on, and then assaulted (sometimes robbed).

It is easy to see the exaggerated behavior that is common in reaction formation and compensation in the above pattern. This is just what the latent homosexual is doing. He is devoting his life to a fight, but the fight is with himself. Because so much time and energy are wasted in this battling, the person is very sensitive to anything or anyone that threatens to expose this hidden aspect of his personality. He can, and frequently does, explode into violent aggressiveness upon the presentation of only a slight provocation.

A latent homosexual finds it difficult to remain faithful to a wife because one woman is just not enough proof of his masculinity. It is no accident that this type of person is called a "man's man."

All latent homosexuals do not behave in the above manner. Many find other ways to compensate. For example, some lose themselves in intellectual pursuits. Their studies serve a dual purpose. First they help to keep the homosexuality suppressed or repressed. Second, these activities give them a feeling of superiority. They do not become involved with the opposite sex because no one can measure up to their expectations. No one is good enough for them.

Pedophilia is a deviancy which involves erotic play with children. It can be heterosexual or homosexual and occasionally includes the rape of a young girl. More often, no penetration is made; instead, an older man fondles or caresses the child. In the case of homosexual pedophilia mouth-genital contact or pederasty may occur.

Actually, cases of pedophilia are quite rare. Many men (and they usually are men) have been arrested when their intent was not sexual at all. Many parents frighten their children, especially their daughters, by constant warnings about the dangers of talking to or riding with strangers. Some of these children have such a rich fantasy concept of the world that the least friendly gesture from a stranger can send them into panic. If the child does panic and start screaming, very few people are going to believe the adult's testimony.

Most people arrested for pedophilia are elderly men. It is extremely doubtful that many of these men intended to harm the child at all. Elderly people live in a shadow world. Their abilities are declining and this shows up in their self-concepts. They are no longer as sure of themselves, as confident, as they once were. Because of this lack of self-confidence, they are likely to withdraw more and more from adults and to seek acquaintance with children. Children are not as threatening; they don't demand as much as adults; they haven't reached the same level of accomplishment. But what happens if any of these children see their advances as sexual advances? The following cases illustrate the point:

> Mr. Brown was a retired gentlemen of 70. Since retirement he had little to do, so he spent much of his time downtown walking the streets. He talked with anyone who had the time to talk to him. Mr. Brown had always loved children so it was natural that many of his contacts were with youngsters. One day he walked up to a parked car in which a preschool child was sitting. He tried to strike up a conversation with the little

boy. The child looked him in the eye and said, "Mister, if you don't move on fast, I am going to start screaming." Nothing happened in this case. But suppose for a moment that the child has been a little girl and that instead of saying what the above child said, she had simply started screaming? What then? It is altogether possible that another "pervert" would have been behind bars.

Little Nancy's parents taught her well. One day her grandmother stopped and offered her a ride home from school. Nancy refused, saying that she could ride home only with her mother or her father. How many "child molesters" live in this child's fantasy world?

In the book *The Lolita Complex,* Trainer (1966) presented a large number of case histories involving real life Lolitas and Humberts. Most of the pedophiles in this book were normal, red-blooded males who were actually seduced by little girls. Many girls learn the art of seduction quite early in life either by direct instruction from their mothers or as a means to gaining favors from a stepfather or a foster parent. It is in this latter situation, involving a male who is not the real father of the child, where most Lolita situations occur. The man gets emotionally entangled with the girl and one day forgets that she is a child.

In actual cases of pedophilia, the pattern is that of a severely disturbed personality. As a group, pedophiles are the most likely of all (with the exception of rapists) to use force on their victims. Frequently, they are severe neurotics or borderline psychotics. Some are mental defectives, and a few of these crimes are perpetrated under the influence of alcohol or drugs. Real life Humberts are often attracted to teaching as a profession, Trainer (1966).

The dynamics of pedophiles are little understood but it seems safe to assume that the majority are immature individuals with deep-seated inferiority and insecurity feelings. They are similar to other sexual deviants in that their overall approach to sex is immature and their deviant behavior is a less threatening outlet than are normal sexual relations.

Because of the physical and psychological damage done to the victims, society deals harshly with the pedophile. Long prison terms are the usual outcome and this is probably as it should be, at least until suitable therapeutic methods are found. At least society is protected when these individuals are behind bars.

Bestiality involves achieving sexual satisfaction by using animals. Masturbation, fellatio, or actual intercourse may be involved. This behavior is not at all uncommon on farms and in rural areas. In fact, in some western states sheep are called "Wyoming prostitutes" or "Kansas golden girls." Almost all large farm animals and domestic pets have been used as sexual objects.

Bestiality usually occurs among boys, but it has been reported among girls, especially with dogs. Farm boys have been known to have intercourse with sheep, goats, cattle, horses, dogs, chickens, ducks, and geese, to name a few. According to Kinsey et al. (1948), about one boy in twelve has had sexual relations with an animal and among farm boys the ratio goes up to approximately 17 per cent.

Bestiality is considered a serious crime in the United States, but it has not always been so classified. Some ancient cultures barred all animal intercourse but others made sex with some animals permissible. This condition should not be classified as a deviancy except in those cases where animals are preferred to humans. In these cases, the same dynamics as in other sexual abnormalities probably apply; that is, the individual has an immature personality and fear and/or insecurity usually underlie the deviant behavior.

Exhibitionism is a condition in which a person derives sexual satisfaction from exposing the genitals or secondary erogenous zones in public. Most reported deviants in this category are male, although the incidence among females may be much higher than the arrests would indicate. Quite often the exposure is accompanied by masturbation and/or other suggestive motions.

Most of the time the exhibitionist follows a standard *modus operandi*. The exposures are at a particular place, perhaps in front of high schools, in department stores, or in theatres, and at a particular time of the day or night. The man will often park in a car and wait for his victim (often a specific physical type within a specified age range) to come along. When the subject comes by, the exhibitionist exposes himself, often asking the question, "Have you ever seen anything like this?" and then speeds off in his car.

Shock on the part of the victim is frequently necessary if the act is to accomplish the excitement that the deviant desires. Apparently one of the purposes of the exhibitionism is to generate excitement. If the victim fails to "sit up and take notice," the exhibitionist may fail to receive sexual satisfaction. For example, Apfelberg et al. (1944) tell of a case where the patient asked his victim if she had ever seen such a large penis, "On one occasion the woman, instead of evidencing shock and embarrassment, looked at him scornfully and assured him that she had. On this occasion the defendant stated that he received no sexual gratification."

Some exhibitionists are not immediately reported. For example:

> A rather handsome 17-year-old boy had been seating himself beside girls and women in darkened theatres and then exhibiting himself and masturbating. He had been repeatedly

successful in obtaining approving collaboration from the women before he finally made the mistake of exposing himself to a policewoman. Out of an estimated 25 to 30 exposures, he was reported only on three occasions. (James C. Coleman, *Abnormal Psychology and Modern Life*, 2nd ed. Chicago: Scott, Foresman & Co., 1956, p. 377.)

Women are less likely to become exhibitionists than are men. When they do, they are rarely reported. Instead of exposing the genitals, exhibitionistic women are more likely to expose other parts of the body, such as the breasts.

Freudian theory seems to supply the best explanation of the dynamics of this condition. Castration anxiety and an unresolved Oedipal situation are apparently at the core of the problem. Exhibitionists are usually immature with regard to their knowledge of and approach to sex. Quite often they show a history of over-attachment to their mothers. The following is a summary of this type of personality formation:

> The exhibitionist, therefore, insofar as this particular activity is concerned, is an infantile individual. Otherwise, of course, he may be well educated, capable, efficient, and even highly moral, but with respect to this particular abnormality he is a child and is under the influence of wishes, impressions, and emotional reactions which had their origin in his childhood. (B. Karpman, "The Psychopathology of Exhibitionism," *Journal of Clinical and Experimental Psycopathy*, vol. 9, pp. 179-225, 1948.)

Often the exhibitionist has strong moral convictions against masturbation and even against his exhibitionism. However, at times, his need to demonstrate his masculinity and potency becomes even stronger than his morals. At such times he will go out and expose himself, but will spend the next few days feeling guilty. In this sense, the exhibitionist is similar to the adolescent who feels that masturbation is wrong but who cannot prevent himself from indulging in this activity once in a while. In neither case is the person oversexed. On the contrary, he is undersexed in the sense that he has an overdeveloped conscience.

When a city has an outbreak of exhibitionism, there is usually a tendency on the part of the citizens to become alarmed. However, the majority of exhibitionists seem to be shy, submissive, harmless people. It is true that some cases of exhibitionism are accompanied by more serious pathology, for example, psychosis or severe neurosis, but there is no reason to assume that exhibitionists as a group are dangerous. Once in a great while, exhibitionism is an expression of a generalized hostility toward the opposite sex or toward society in general, but these cases seem to be the exception rather than the rule.

Voyeurism (scotophilia, or inspectionalism) refers to a sexual deviation in which the person receives sexual satisfaction through peeping. The common term for a person in this category is peeping Tom.

When peeping can be called a deviancy among males is open to question. Almost any man or boy, given the opportunity, will look. This is quite evident from the popularity of "girlie" shows, stag movies, and "girlie" magazines in the United States. On the other hand, females, as a general rule, are rather uninterested in peeping (except the very young) and often find it rather hard to understand the voyeuristic tendencies of men. Many conflicts in marriage seem to center around the male's interest in looking and the female's conditioned reluctance to expose her body. If married people are going to satisfy the needs of their mates, it is essential that these different viewpoints toward viewing the body be understood. Some sort of compromise can be worked out if both individuals are willing to try.

Abnormal voyeurism probably results when the individual is so shy and inadequate that he cannot make contact with or have a satisfactory relationship with the opposite sex. By peeping, and frequently masturbating, the individual can partially satisfy his sex needs without the discomfort of approaching the opposite sex. In addition, the suspense and excitement involved in the activity probably have some value as sexual outlets, just as in exhibitionism, kleptomania, or pyromania.

As with exhibitionists, voyeurists are rarely dangerous. In fact they are more likely to be hurt by their victims, who frequently catch them or set traps for them. If they are caught, it is not at all unusual for them to be seriously injured because of the general emotionality that they generate in a neighborhood.

Once in a great while, voyeurism is accompanied by more serious pathology but, as a rule, voyeurists are immature, shy, submissive people with strong feelings of insecurity and inferiority. Most of them have a strong conscience with regard to sex or an exceptionally strong fear of the opposite sex.

Fetishism refers to a deviation in which a person derives sexual satisfaction from some body part other than the genitals or from some object. Frequently, the object is an article of clothing (often the undergarments) of the opposite sex though the fetish may become attached to anything. A few examples of fetish objects are: feet, toes, legs, hair, fingernails, breasts, shoes, socks, panties, brassiers, cigarette butts, pictures of nudes, hair ribbons, perfume, and handkerchiefs. The individual with a fetish receives gratification by kissing, licking, chewing, wearing, caressing, or smelling the object.

Smell was mentioned last in this sequence because of its special importance in emotions. Of all the senses, olfaction is the most primitive and the most closely related to the emotional centers of the brain. It is no coincidence that women's perfumes have such names as "My Sin," "Evening in Paris," and "Intoxication." Fetishes often involve smelling as the mode of sexual satisfaction. This fact gives some insight into the dynamics of some cases of fetishism, in which the individual is responding at a very infantile level of sexual stimulation.

In everyday life, examples of fetishism are rather common. A good example is the reaction of teen-age girls to the Beatles some years ago. Many of these girls showed an almost pathological desire to get parts of clothing or other objects that have been associated with this singing group. Cigarette butts, ashtrays, and other objects left behind in the hotel rooms of the Beatles have brought some fantastic prices.

Some people with a fetish are more interested in the method of obtaining the object than in the object itself. If stealing is for the purpose of sexual pleasure, as it frequently is, the condition is labeled as fetishistic *kleptomania*. As with several types of sexual deviation, the excitement involved in the act may be enough to give the person sexual gratification. This type of fetishism is more frequently associated with women than are other types. However, kleptomania is not confined to women and all cases of kleptomania are not fetishistic.

Although most cases of fetishism are people with an immature approach to and understanding of sex (and therefore relatively harmless), some show behavior associated with more extensive maladjustment. Some cases show a progression from rather harmless types of fetishism to more severe types of pathology. The following case illustrates this point quite vividly:

Some years ago, the police of our large cities were baffled by three sadistic murders which occurred with no evidence of monetary or other clear-cut motivation. On the wall of one apartment, in which an ex-Wave was brutally killed, there appeared in lipstick "For heaven's sake, catch me before I kill more: I cannot control myself." In another killing a child of six was kidnapped and her body dismembered and thrown into various sewers and drains. The kidnapper wrote and delivered a ransom note to the child's parents. No progress was made in this until a policeman off duty captured a young man who was trying to make a getaway after an attempt at burglary. The boy would probably have been released on probation had it not been for an alert police official who noticed a resemblance between a curve flourish in the boy's signature and the ransom note. This boy, a 17-year-old university student, proved to be the perpetrator of these crimes.

The events leading up to these shocking murders by this youth have been carefully studied by psychiatrists and psychologists and the following points from the clinical report on this case are of considerable value in showing the dynamics in sexual sadism as well as in other sexual deviations. The boy was found to be of normal intelligence, not psychotic, and medically normal; electroencephalographic tracings were normal.

When aged 9, the patient began to be interested in the "feeling and color" and then "the stealing" of women's underclothing. He began to take these at first from clotheslines, then from basements, and later from strange houses, the doors of which he found open or ajar. Dresses or other articles of woman's apparel made no appeal to him nor was he interested in the undergarments of his immediate family. Having secured a pair of women's panties or drawers, he would take it to a basement or home, put it on, experience excitement and sexual completion. Most garments he then threw away, some he replaced, and some he hoarded.

When 12 or 13 years of age, he secured the desired garments by going into houses through windows. This furnished more excitement. After three such expeditions, he took objects (guns or money) other than underclothes; a change which was again an added stimulation. "It seemed sort of foolish to break in and not take anything." When he had thus changed his objective, the interest in underclothes largely evaporated and was replaced by the excitement experienced on making an entrance through the window. Often he would struggle against his desire to leave his room at night, but when he did leave, it was for the purpose of committing burglaries. He had sexual excitement or an erection at the sight of an open window at the place to be burglarized. Going through the window he had an emission.

Even after his admission to the university, this deviate behavior continued, although it apparently became increasingly difficult to achieve sexual gratification, and it took several entrances to produce an emission. On one occasion he was startled in the act of burglarizing by a nurse whom he promptly struck and injured. This resulted in an orgasm, and he left without striking her again and returned to his room at the university. On subsequent occasions when he was startled in the course of his burglarizing, he immediately killed. In one instance he had an erection on entering the house and "the dog barked and the lady started hollering. She had on a nightgown. She jumped up and hollered. Then I took the knife and stabbed her — through the throat — just to keep her quiet." Although this resulted in an orgasm he apparently had not intended to kill the woman. "It was the noise that set me off, I believe. I must have been in a high tension and the least bit of noise would disturb me in that manner."

After an emission was the only time he felt he had done wrong . . . [Then he suffered] from the pang of conscience. This compelling urge had clearly a dynamic sexual origin . . . so we asked him had he never relieved this tension by manual manipulation. On one occasion he indignantly denied even the attempt . . . Later he said he tried this method twice without success. In the same manner he at first denied ever having attempted any sex play with girls. Two days later with one of his rare shows of emotion he said, looking much ashamed, that twice, later correcting himself to eight times, he had touched girls "on the breasts" and then pressed "on the leg." Always, having done this, he would immediately burst into tears and "be upset and unable to sleep." He forcibly denied ever having made any more intimate advances, except that he "kissed them" sometimes. "They wanted to kiss; I didn't."

It was clear that normal sex stimulation and experience were unpleasant, indeed repulsive, to him, and these efforts afterwards created in him a negative emotional state. He found them improper in the conduct of others; he never spoke of them except in condemnation . . . (Adapted from F. Kennedy, H. R. Hoffman, and W. H. Haines, "A Study of William Heirens," *American Journal of Psychiatry,* vol. 104, pp. 113-21, 1947.)

Pyromania refers to the firebug, a person who has a compulsive urge to set fires. Quite often this person receives sexual pleasure from the burning, which parenthetically is associated frequently in everyday language with passion, as well as from the excitement generated by the milling spectators. This reaction is closely related to fetishism in that fire becomes the inanimate object for sexual gratification and the dynamics are similiar; the individual is using infantile approaches to satisfying his sexual drives. The causes are varied, but, in general, the usual explanations will suffice. Pyromaniacs are immature, insecure people who find normal sexual relations threatening or who have such a strong fear of the opposite sex that a sexual advance toward another person is impossible. Fire becomes a symbolic substitute for passion and excitement.

Pyromaniacs are a menace to society in that the fires they set destroy property and even occasionally, lives. However, it is doubtful that sending them to prison is beneficial to society or to the individual. These people need psychotherapy to help them overcome their anxiety and to encourage them to have normal human relationships.

Necrophilia involves having intercourse with a dead person, or in some cases an orgasm may be achieved through fondling, caressing, or even viewing a human corpse. Where female necrophiles are reported, the condition has to involve something other than sexual intercourse.

Cases of necrophilia are extremely rare and usually involve severe behavior pathology other than the perversion itself. The usual dynamics probably apply, that is, fear or repulsion of sex. Dead people do not present a threat of hindered or disturbed interpersonal relationships. The choice of sexual object is about as safe as one could find. Of course, the aversion society has for corpses creates an emotionally charged situation for anyone caught indulging in this behavior. Because this attitude is so prevalent, the necrophile must be out of touch with society in order to indulge in the deviant response.

Sadism involves the receiving of sexual pleasure by inflicting pain on others. Sadists may be homosexual, heterosexual, or bisexual. Some sadists combine this deviancy with fetishism; some object rather than a person is mutilated or destroyed. The perversion varies all the way from a normal amount of roughness, such as biting and clawing in lovemaking, to a few cases in which the victim is slain and then brutally mutilated. In fact, sadists vary so much that one can question whether or not all should be placed in the same category.

There is only common feature to all types of sadism, when the term is used to denote sexual deviation, and that is the linking of sex and aggression. This usage is somewhat understandable because these two emotions are often linked even in normal sexual relationships. Boys talk about the conquest of a girl. Many people develop a stronger sexual appetite when they are angry. Married couples say, "The fun of the breakup is the makeup." An everyday expression, "All's fair in love and war," illustrates well the sex-aggression association.

The term sadism was derived from the Marquis de Sade (1740-1814) who, while in prison for sexual deviation, wrote the most comprehensive book on perversions which has ever been written. Many of the deviations involved violence in one form or another. Whether Sade ever engaged in actual sadistic behavior is debatable. The writings of the Marquis demonstrate the wide range of behavior that can be considered sadistic. It can vary from verbal abuse through smearing the victim with noxious chemicals to murder and mutilation of the sexual partner. There is really no limit to how extreme sadistic behavior can become.

Most sadists are men; however, the condition is not confined to the male. The biting, scratching, clawing, and neck-sucking behavior of some women can be considered as examples of a minor deviation. Homosexuals, both male and female, can be brutal in their sexual activities.

The dynamics of sadism are probably varied. It seems likely that the Christian association between sex and sin produces some sadists. People are quick to condemn others for behavior they themselves practice. It is easy to rationalize our own behavior because, after all, we do have a legitimate excuse. But to excuse the behavior of others is much more difficult because we cannot appreciate their reasons for behaving as they do. Therefore, some sadists are probably punishing their sexual partners for what they consider to be sinful actions. They may justify their behavior by reasoning that they are proving to the victim just how evil sex is.

A more probable explanation of the dynamics of sadism is that the perversion is merely part of a more generalized hostility toward humanity. Freud pointed out in

Totem and Taboo (1913) and *The Future of an Illusion* (1927) the very process of civilization is such that some hostility is produced toward mankind. In becoming civilized one has to give up some of his freedom.

Aggression is often used by the representatives of society to force one to do things that he does not want to do, or vice versa. Inevitably, a socialized human has developed a great amount of hostility by the time he has become civilized. Because most cultures limit the expression of aggression, much of this hostility is kept submerged at the unconscious level. The person learns to repress aggressive emotions, especially those directed toward certain situations. This hostility remains active at the unconscious level and is there to guide behavior even though the person is unaware of why he acts the way he does.

The guilt created by sexual feelings can produce hostile emotions toward the person who causes the erotic arousal. The projected impulse takes the form, "It's not my fault. It is yours. And you must be punished for making me indulge in this sinful act." This type of case is illustrated by a case study reported by Wertham (1949). In this case, the sadist killed and mutilated young girls and castrated adolescent boys. He rationalized his behavior by reasoning that he was protecting them from future immoral acts. (Adapted from Coleman, 1964).

Sadistic behavior as merely part of a more complex pattern of psychopathology is often reported. In psychotic episodes, there is a general lowering of inhibitions and morals. If a person is predisposed in an antisocial direction, the reduced inhibitions can lead to an increase in both sexual and aggressive behavior. In addition, the lack of touch with reality and a corresponding reduced awareness of social responsibility may produce a quite complex sadistic situation. This type of situation is complicated even further by the frequent use of alcohol and narcotics by borderline psychotics and psychotics. Such a sadist may be totally unaware of what he is doing. In some cases, he is doing what the voices tell him to do.

Another explanation of sadism is that it is the result of early learning. Many children have witnessed their parents or others in the act of sexual intercourse. The act itself can be viewed as an aggressive action in which the father is assaulting the mother. This, linked with the generalizing character of emotions, can condition a sadistic approach to erotic feelings. Simple and complex conditioning probably accounts for much deviant behavior.

A Freudian viewpoint of sadism states that this condition grows out of castration anxiety. One of the real problems of latent homosexuality is the tendency to indulge in exaggerated behavior. A man with severe doubts about his masculinity can easily adopt a manner of trying to show women that he is a man.

Since aggression is identified as a masculine characteristic in North American society, it seems natural to expect a shy, effeminate man to become somewhat sadistic if he is going to prove his manhood to others as well as to himself. If the sadistic behavior arouses strong emotions in the partner and is thereby rewarded, it is more likely to be incorporated into the person's habit system.

Some individuals can respond sexually only when they are feeling hostile. This attitude combined with a felt need to compensate for real or imagined inadequacies can lead to a sado-masochistic situation in which emotions have to be created through some form of brutality.

Masochism is defined as a sexual deviation in which the individual receives sexual satisfaction only when the sex act is associated with pain. Some individuals prefer verbal abuse, whereas others seek actual physical assault. The types of torture can be as varied as the individuals themselves. Some variations are being whipped, tied up, paddled, switched, stuck with pins, or cut with knives. The term itself comes from an Austrian novelist Leopold Von Sacher-Masoch (1836-1895) whose fictional characters derive sexual satisfaction from all sorts of cruel situations.

Masochists may be heterosexual, homosexual, or bisexual. In many large cities in the United States, certain bars are designated as "leather" bars. These lounges serve as a gathering place for homosexuals who are also interested in sado-masochistic activities. A large number of contact publications are now available for people who want to correspond and meet "unusual" people. Ads in these guides run somewhat as follows: "Dominant Dame, 35, 5'9", 175 lbs., 40-31-38. Would like to hear from others who are interested in leather, *discipline*." A picture is shown of a massive woman dressed as a circus lion tamer, wearing leather gloves, and holding a whip. Another advertisement reads as follows: "Beautiful young and dominant woman. Interests varied; leather and rubber garments, ladies' undergarments, domestic discipline, etc." The photograph shows an attractive young woman wearing a leather mask and holding a long switch. The following illustrates the masochistic side: "Male, 30 and obedient. Will be servant to any aggressive woman, 20-35. Race no barrier."

Some masochism is probably anchored in the Christian-Victorian assumption that there is value in suffering. The trials and tribulations of Job are presented as a model. Supposedly, the more we suffer on earth, the better our chances in the next life. This theory, combined with a link between sex and sin, has led some individuals to feel that any pleasure, especially sexual pleasure, is worldly and sinful.

The guilt which is engendered leads to an unbearable inner conflict. These people have a sex drive which must be fulfilled, but they must be punished for their sin. They are like the little boy forbidden to go swimming who brings a switch to his mother and says, "Go ahead and switch me now and get it over with because I *am* going swimming." They are willing to pay the immediate price rather than wait for the more expensive price of extreme guilt later on.

Often, parents who are unbending in their teaching of moral and religious values are also cold and aloof toward their children. The children not only are told that sex is dirty, vulgar, and sinful; they also learn that the only way they can receive attention is to misbehave.

Negative attention is better than no attention at all. The generalizing capacity of the human mind could lead such people to equate pain and torture with affection and attention. Many college males proudly display scratches on their back and passion marks to their peers in the dormitory.

The Freudian explanation of masochism is that it is a reaction formation to unconscious sadistic impulses. This viewpoint seems to have merit for two reasons: (1) most masochists are women and, (2) some of the most brutal sex crimes are perpetuated by individuals who showed a previous history of masochism.

Girls, even more so than boys, are taught to repress their aggressive impulses. Theoretically, the more anger is repressed, the greater the chance that it will turn into hostility, and the more the hostility will build up. If this happens, there is a possibility that a volcano of emotions is boiling around just below the surface. Anyone who has ever witnessed a fight between two women knows that their style differs from fisticuffs between men. When they do reach the point of physical violence, they are more likely to show the killer instinct.

If unconscious hostility is a constant threat to the integrity of the person, one way that he can keep it in check is to become the wounded rather than the aggressor. This is not too different from a situation in which an individual experiences psychological "hurt." If we examine closely the times that we have experienced psychological injury, most of the time, the situation was one in which anger would have been a more appropriate response. For example, our girl friend "hurts" us deeply by deserting us or by going out with someone else. We sit around indulging in self-pity and licking our wounds. We really should be angry, but aggressive responses to those we love are bad. Since we are not bad, these feelings cannot possibly be permitted. Instead, we repress our anger and suffer as in the following case:

> Barbara was a brilliant student who showed many signs of personal and social maladjustment. She remained alone most of the time and had great difficulty in communicating when she was in a group.
>
> It was noticed that quite often she would come to class with deep fingernail scratches on her arms and legs. After months of counseling (when good rapport had been established) she was asked about the scratches. She admitted that she scratched herself when she felt sexually frustrated. The wounds had autoerotic significance to her. Scratching took the place of masturbation.
>
> Barbara developed a crush on one of her male professors. At first he was sympathetic and made a great effort to help her develop more social grace and desirable personal qualities. He introduced her to groups of students and worked for her acceptance in the groups. For a while, things seemed to be working out just right. She was being accepted by more and

more people. She was invited to join into many activities from which she was previously banned.

Barbara grew more and more demanding of the time of her teacher. She would follow him around everywhere he went. She waited outside his classes so that she could talk with him for a few minutes. During his off hours she was always there. Then she began to drop by his house at night. The entire situation grew more and more embarrassing for the professor. At last he had to reject her in no uncertain terms. She was instructed to stay away from him at all times.

This girl then began a campaign of espionage against her previous love. She was going to get even with him by prying into his personal life. For months she waited outside his house in the dark trying to dig up something that would get him into trouble. This approach was unsuccessful, so one black night she physically assaulted the professor. As a result, Barbara was forced to withdraw from college.

This case illustrates some of the points made earlier. The girl came from a home where the parents were much older than usual. They were rigid and unbending in their religious and moral teachings. Barbara was never allowed to date while she was at home, and because of gross personal and social maladjustment, she was never asked for a date in college. She had never had any sexual experience except an autoerotic masochistic experience. When wounded personally by her only love, she became a vicious animal. Years later she repeated the entire sequence at another college.

Many masochists probably learn their behavior in a straightforward manner. Some mothers teach their daughters to expect pain in sexual intercourse by direct example. Others are taught a pain-sex association by listening to their mothers talk to other women. The extreme pain of their first intercourse often strengthens a belief that it is a woman's lot in life to suffer. Relatives and neighbors can reinforce this attitude.

Mass media portray situations in which excitement

and pain are associated. Some learning theorists, for example, Thorndike (1911 and 1932), have emphasized that humans can learn to like pain if it is associated often enough with something pleasurable. In addition, the human mind is a generalizing mind. Other stimuli occuring in conjunction with pleasant situations can take on secondary reinforcing characteristics.

Kraines (1948) reported a case that seems to support this conditioning theory. The patient could experience a sexual orgasm only if the intercourse were accompanied by a spanking with a ruler. In tracing the origin of this condition, Kraines found that it began when, as an adolescent, the patient was placed across the knees of a much admired, in fact much loved, female teacher for the purpose of being punished. She spanked him with a ruler but in the process he had an orgasm because of the close physical contact.

In summary, the phrase sexual deviation covers a variety of behaviors, some of which seem truly perverted. Others depend to a large extent upon the perceiver. What is acceptable in one culture or subculture may be condemned in another. The deviations listed in this discussion should not be taken as a definitive list, nor should all of them be considered as *bad* deviations. They are merely behavior patterns that have been called deviant in the Judaeo-Christian tradition.

The Puritanical approach to sexual education has been a threat approach. Children and adolescents have been continually reminded of the three dangers: conception, infection, and detection. Is it any wonder that many people grow to fear normal heterosexual contact? Is it a mystery why some find a less threatening sexual substitution? As was previously discussed, the substitution may be much worse than the real act.

The causes of sexual deviation are probably varied

but most psychologists agree that the behavior is learned, not inborn. If behavior is learned, then it can be unlearned. This is exactly the approach that is employed in behavior therapy. Inappropriate responses are punished and appropriate responses are positively reinforced.

Thus far, conditioning therapy has been more successful in treating sexual deviation than any other form of psychotherapy. For example, one researcher has said that everything about a rapist's behavior is appropriate except his mode of attack. All the rapist needs to know is how to seduce women and he will no longer need to rape. So this experimenter has proceeded to teach his patients the art of seduction. The method seems to be working.

Because the sexually deviant individual is often ridiculed, abused, and maligned, the sexual behavior can become the center of the person's life. He may be hired or fired on the basis of his behavior. He may be scorned, assaulted, or rejected by certain groups. He has to be cautious in talking to others. He may be blackmailed, divorced, or abandoned. All of these things, plus many other things that could happen to him, may lead to a preoccupation. This in turn can trap the person in a neurotic vicious circle in which more personality maladjustment becomes evident. If this happens, then simply changing the sexual behavior could lead to drastic changes in overall personality. This is the assumption of the behavior therapist and, so far, the results of this approach seem encouraging.

4
alcoholism
and drug addiction

Figures are quoted in various books stating that there are from one million to six million alcoholics in the United States. These figures relate only to the hopeless alcoholics, not to the millions of other people who are heavy drinkers, but who still somehow manage to keep their jobs, to keep their families together, and to maintain some degree of respectability. There is little doubt that alcoholism is a major social problem in America. It is estimated that about half of all highway fatalities are alcohol related.

Two criteria are used to determine whether or not a person is considered a chronic alcoholic: (1) if the use of alcohol leads to severe interference in social, personality, or physical functioning and (2) if the person has an obsessive desire and compulsion to drink regardless of the consequences. In the first of these, the person usually loses job after job because of his drinking, gets into great trouble with his family and friends, gets into trouble with the law, loses prestige in the community, and harms himself physically one way or another (through improper diet, overexposure, or by drinking liquids which have toxic elements in addition to the alcohol).

In the second criterion, once the person takes a drink, he must continue to drink until he loses consciousness, runs out of money, gets thrown in jail, or is stopped by some external agent. He cannot stop drinking of his own volition. This individual is either unable to recognize the harmful effects of his drinking or, if he does recognize the effects, he is unable to stop his drinking.

In addition to the chronic alcoholics, there are millions of problem drinkers in the United States. The problem drinker may consume as much or more alcohol than the alcoholic but he has some semblance of control. He can maintain his occupation, stop drinking when it is time to go to bed, and even stop drinking when he recognizes the problems his behavior has caused.

Many individuals have been taught that alcohol is a poison. On the contrary, ethyl alcohol (C_2H_5OH) is a high energy food organically similar to the simple sugars, for example, glucose ($C_6H_{12}O_6$). Alcohol can be utilized by the body at a rate of about one ounce per hour. One of the problems of the alcoholic is that he may come to depend more and more on the alcohol as a food and consequently neglect eating properly.

The alcohol cannot supply many of the necessary nutrients, especially the vitamins. The B-complex vitamins are needed daily (they cannot be stored in the body) for proper nervous system functioning. Nerve cells, unlike other cells in the body, cannot regenerate. If they are not fed properly, permanent nervous system damage can occur. It is now believed that many of the symptoms of alcohol-produced psychoses are the result of B-complex vitamin deficiency.

Another popular misconception about alcohol is that

it is a stimulant. In actuality, alcoholic beverages act as a depressant. The apparent stimulating effects are due to lowered inhibitions. Most people feel sleepy after a few drinks but if they continue to drink they seem to wake up and want to continue indefinitely. The functioning of the higher brain centers is altered so that the behavior of the individual begins to change.

Some of these behavioral changes are due to the physical properties of the alcohol but some changes seem to be of psychological origin. For example, the author once gave a party at which nothing but nonalcoholic champagne was served. Most of the people at the party showed some signs of intoxication and some showed extreme symptoms.

The psychological feelings that the individual experiences depend upon a variety of factors, such as his inhibitions, the people with whom he is associated, the emotional climate in which the drinking occurs, the purpose for drinking, recent pleasant or unpleasant experiences, etc. Most people drink to escape unpleasant realities and consequently try to have a good time. These persons experience a feeling of euphoria, warmth, increased confidence, joviality, comraderie, well-being, etc. Others have inhibited their aggressive impulses to the point that when their inhibitions are lowered, they become belligerent and hostile. These people are referred to as "fighting drunks."

There is no evidence to indicate that alcohol permanently affects any organ in the body except the liver. When an alcoholic beverage is ingested, the body begins at once to utilize the alcohol through a process of oxidation. About 10 per cent is lost through breathing, urination, perspiration, etc. The remainder accumulates until it can be oxidized.

One highball (1½ oz. of whisky) or two twelve-ounce

beers will produce a concentration of about 0.03% in the bloodstream of a 150-pound man. He will experience only a slight change in feelings and it will take about two hours for the alcohol to leave the body. Three highballs, six bottles of beer, or a pint of wine raises the concentration level to 0.09%. This is quite near to the 0.10% point, which, in most states, is defined as the legal limit of intoxication.

The person experiences a feeling of buoyancy or moroseness. He usually exaggerates emotions and is often talkative, noisy, or sullen. The body requires about six hours to oxidize this amount of alcohol. Coordination is usually hindered at this point. The person may stagger when he walks and his sense of balance is hindered in other ways. His speech pattern is disturbed. He begins to slur some of his words.

Five cocktails, ten bottles of beer, a fifth of wine, or a half-pint of whisky produces unmistakable intoxication in the average-sized man. The blood concentration level is usually about 0.15%. At 0.5% most people pass out. This is fortunate because a concentration level above this is usually fatal.

The fact that an individual can die from an overdose of alcohol probably accounts for the misconception that it is toxic. However, it is not the toxic properties, but the depressant properties of alcohol that produce death. Nor does alcohol cook the brain as is often demonstrated to adolescents by dropping a raw egg into ethyl alcohol.

Most people start drinking in a similar manner, that is, as a means to social intercourse. They find that alcohol has tension-reducing properties. By drinking, they can reduce some of the everyday frustrations, irritations, and disappointments. They find a temporary escape from the realities of a conflict-producing world. In addition, there are some social, personal, and at times, even occupational advantages in attending cocktail parties. Many people are able to limit their alcohol consumption to special occasions, but others are not.

The person who is ultimately to become an alcoholic soon finds himself trapped in a neurotic vicious circle. He finds more and more excuses to drink: he needs to relax after a hard day at the office; he wants to celebrate the arrival or departure of a friend; his wife doesn't understand him; it is Friday and payday; the children are driving him crazy; his wife nags all of the time; he is lonesome and wants to meet some friends; he wants to pick up a woman; he is being held back on the job.

Alcohol has become an anxiety reducer but it will eventually produce more anxiety, which in turn will have to be reduced by taking another drink. Gradually the individual's tolerance for alcohol builds up. It now takes more drinks to achieve the same effects. He starts the afternoon or evening with some concentrated combination of beverages, such as a double shot and beer chaser, a "boilermaker," or an extra-dry martini. After the initial "shocker," he settles back to more or less normal drinking.

Usually, the person reaches a point where he is subject to black outs, in which he cannot remember what happened after the first one or two drinks. The black out seems to serve two purposes: (1) it prevents him from knowing how much he had to drink, and (2) it reduces guilt and shame for any unacceptable act he may have committed while under the influence.

Normally, by this time, the incipient alcoholic has started to stock a supply. If he is going to a party, he has a drink or two before going because "there may not be enough to go around." Drinking is beginning to become the center of his life. He is preoccupied with beverages, parties, and protecting his supply. If he is single, he begins to associate more and more with drinking buddies. If he is married and cannot get his wife involved in his whirlwind, he will find excuses to work late, to go out with the boys, or he will begin to hide some of his supply so that he can sneak a few extra drinks without his wife's knowledge.

The man (and man is used here because most alcoholics are male though the incidence among women is rapidly increasing) is now well on his way to becoming an alcoholic. He starts to drink earlier and earlier during the day, often having a couple of drinks in the morning to brace himself for the day. By this time he is often in trouble at work because of absenteeism, reduced performance, coming to work drunk or severly hung over; also, problems in the family and with friends and neighbors are growing rapidly.

These increased problems cause the person to want to drink even more so that he can escape what has now become an ever-increasingly hostile and threatening world. At this point the individual stops talking about drinking and parties and takes elaborate steps to hide from others the amount of alcohol he consumes each day.

Sometime during this period, he will probably get into trouble with the law. He will be jailed once, or as is more often the case, many times. His troubles are multiplying. His family and friends have lost patience with him; he has lost his job or is in jeopardy of losing it; he has a criminal record. But he will still deny that he is an alcoholic. He will affirm that "I can stop anytime I want to."

All of these troubles severly weaken the person's self-respect and confidence. He is becoming vaguely aware that he can no longer control his drinking; the drinking controls him. In many cases the pattern of his acquaintances begins to change. People of inferior status or class are sought as companions. This allows the alcoholic to maintain a trace of integrity, a minute feeling of superiority. By this time the person has normally been abandoned by his family and most of his previous associates.

Where this does not happen, the wife, consciously or unconsciously, is often a force in keeping the alcoholism going. Any number of interactive reasons may be involved. The wife may enjoy being a martyr because of the attention and sympathy she receives from others; she may enjoy seeing her husband helpless because this proves that all men are no good; her husband's condition may provide her with a weapon in securing her children as allies.

Toward the end of this period, most alcoholics reach a point where their tolerance for alcohol is reduced. It now takes less for them to get drunk. Often they have been reduced to nothingness; they have no family, job, friends, or money. They may start drinking anything that has alcohol in it: antiseptic, shaving lotion, shoe polish strained through bread, or lotions. Others move into skid row districts and beg a few meager pennies for the purchase of cheap wine. They sleep in alleys, doorways, flophouses, or in jail. They use every cent they can get to purchase something to drink.

Not all alcoholics follow all of the steps listed above but all reach a point where alcohol is in total control of their behavior. Wealthy people may become alcoholic without the social repercussions of the average man. Usually though, an alcoholic will have to hit rock bottom before he will admit that he is an alcoholic and consequently seek help. What started out to be an anxiety reducer has now placed the individual in a situation in which there is unlimited anxiety produced by the behavior.

Many studies have been done in an effort to establish some physical causation for alcoholism. To date the experiments have been unsuccessful. The cause and effect relationship is at best hazy and ill-defined. There probably are some constitutional differences in metabolism, but physiology as a primary cause of this condition has almost been ruled out. Instead, many authorities feel that the psychological state of the individual is of primary importance.

Most alcoholics can be described as inadequate personalities; they usually have a poor self-concept and have trouble accepting the frustrations and conflicts of the real world. Instead, they reduce anxiety and dull emotions in the fantasy world of alcohol. Even when they are not drinking, they cannot be described as adequate because they are still faced with the conflict of not wanting to accept reality. There is an inner battle between what is real and what is fantasy.

Alcoholism is no respecter of social status. Alcoholics are found in all socioeconomic classes and in every trade, occupation, and profession. The condition is more common in men than among women, but the incidence in females has shown rapid increases in recent years. There do appear to be differences between various subcultures within the United States, the percentages being low in Jewish and Italian groups and high in Irish and French subcultures. Figures from around the world fluctuate from one year to the next, but the United States almost always ranks among the top three.

Alcohol related psychoses

There are five types of psychotic conditions which result from prolonged or excessive use of alcoholic beverages: (1) pathologic intoxication, (2) delirium tremens, (3) alcoholic hallucinosis, (4) Korsakoff's syndrome (or psychosis), and (5) alcoholic dementia. *Pathologic intoxication* is also called mania a potu. Many people have a low tolerance for alcohol. This is especially true in certain types of disease or after some types of brain injury. Also there are times, as during fatigue or after missing one or several meals, when anyone may have a lowered threshold. When this happens, the person may manifest extremely aggressive and violent behavior after a few drinks. Some of these cases of alcoholic fury have even led to homicide. Usually after several hours of this extreme behavior the individual falls into a deep sleep and cannot remember the incident at all the next day. This condition is called pathologic intoxication.

The following case history, though not truly classical of the syndrome, represents many aspects of this condition:

The patient, a 35-year-old professional man, reported to the psychiatrist because of "four or five" instances in which he had physically and verbally assaulted his wife. On the surface, he was a mild-mannered, soft-spoken individual who appeared in the psychiatrist's office gently holding his three-year-old daughter. He had come to the psychiatrist because he could not understand his unusual behavior "at these times." He was actually very fond of his wife and children and "wanted to save his marriage."

After preliminary conversation, the patient was sent to a local hospital for an EEG (electroencephalogram) and a complete neurological examination. The first EEG showed abnormal brain activity which could not be localized from the gross recording. A second and more thorough EEG indicated abnormal brainwave activity in the temporal lobe. Nothing pathological was found in the neurological examination.

In trying to establish a cause and effect relationship, the patient was asked about his drinking habits because he had already stated that these aggressive episodes came while he was drinking. In recalling his past, the patient remembered that even before his marriage the episodes had always come during a period when he was drinking on a day-to-day basis. This man was not alcoholic in the sense that he had experienced periods of steady drinking and long dry periods in between. The regular drinking was always correlated to some externally frustrating situation, for example, being in the Army, and friction developing in his marriage. Even in the steady drinking periods, he did not consume large amounts of alcohol. He would drink two or three beers after getting home from work. There were occasional parties in which the volume increased.

The neurologist and the psychiatrist jointly concluded that alcohol had a cummulative toxic effect on this patient because of temporal lobe brain injury and that he could control his aggressive, hostile behavior simply by reserving his drinking for special occasions, such as social gatherings and parties. He was instructed to refrain from having the two or three beers every night. Three years later, there had been no additional violent episodes.

This case does not represent every symptom in the pathologic intoxication syndrome because this patient could remember what he did the night before. He not only could remember but he was also remorseful and apologetic for weeks after the episode.

Delirium tremens is a condition commonly referred to as the DT's. After years of habitual drinking, the alcoholic may develop these familiar psychotic symptoms. The entire syndrome includes (1) coarse tremors, (2) disorientation, (3) intense and animated hallucination, (4) an anxiety reaction, and (5) marked suggestibility. Usually, there are other physiological symptoms such as perspiration, fever, or a fast heartbeat, accompanying the major and more pronounced symptoms. Every policeman, jailkeeper, and hospital worker witnesses this disturbance at one time or another.

As the second part of the name for this condition would suggest, one of the most notable of the symptoms is the gross trembling that occurs in the patient. These tremors usually involve the fingers, hands, arms, face, mouth, and tongue. This uncontrollable shaking and trembling goes on for hours or days and is the most readily observable phenomenon even to a novice. This state is often portrayed in movies about alcoholics and most people find it a very alarming experience to witness these "shakes."

Disorientation in time and space is usually pronounced at the height of delirium. The patient cannot concentrate and there is a marked loss of memory, especially for recent events. The disorientation is complicated by the high degree of suggestibility. The person may be led to believe almost anything.

The hallucinations usually are of visual nature, though auditory and tactile hallucinations are sometimes reported. Contrary to popular opinion, alcoholics rarely if ever see pink elephants. Most often the visual hallucinations involve insects or small, fast-moving animals. Cockroaches, rats, and snakes seem to be the most common. Sometimes the individual will feel these animals moving about on his body.

These haptic hallucinations may, in some cases, be the result of biochemical changes within the individual or may be an illusion brought on by the extreme suggestibility of the person. When auditory hallucinations occur, they are usually viewed as a poor prognostic sign. Treatment will probably be prolonged. These false perceptions most often involve self-depreciation, a self-derogatory voice, or someone or something encouraging the patient to indulge in sexually deviant behavior.

Most alcoholics find the hallucinations and illusions

extremely frightening, but a few appear to be totally indifferent. The usual situation is for the patient to experience acute and intense free-floating anxiety in the midst of the delirium. Almost anything can induce pronounced fear reactions. This in combination with extreme suggestibility can lead to a highly volatile situation. Delirium tremens normally last from three to six days. The full-blown syndrome is often preceded by an inability to go to sleep, restlessness, hyperactivity, headaches, fever, rapid pulse, a feeling of dryness in the mouth and throat, profuse perspiration, and a generalized feeling of anxiety, apprehension, uneasiness, and guilt. The fatality rate usually runs around three to four per cent. About 15 percent show progressive pathology to Korsakoff's psychosis.

Both delirium tremens and Korsakoff's syndrome involve nerve cell degeneration. The amount of nervous system damage varies greatly from one patient to the next. The extent of the damage determines, to a large extent, the physiological prognosis. Physical treatment usually consists of large doses of B-complex vitamins. If nerve cells are in the beginning stages of deterioration, they can be restored to normal functioning. If total degeneration has occurred, no medical therapy will do any good because, unlike other cells in the body, many neurons can never be regenerated.

Acute alcoholic hallucinations, unlike the hallucinations in delirium tremens, are marked by auditory misperceptions which are characteristic of this condition. Also unlike the auditory hallucinations in many other forms of psychosis, the voices are talking about the patient, not to him. These voices usually expose his innermost sins or sinful desires and prescribe all sorts of horrible punishments. Most often, the sin is of a sexual nature. The second characteristic of this syndrome is anxiety. The patient may panic at the least provocation.

In alcoholic hallucinosis, in contrast to the DT's, the individual normally remains fairly well oriented in time and space and memory losses are not common. This probably gives rise to the often observed fact that patients in this state fluctuate from anxiety at one moment to humor at the next. At times, the individual seems to recognize the absurdity of the hallucinations and at other times he may be totally terror-stricken. There is something tragically humorous about the entire episode. The voices may continue, off and on, for days and sometimes even weeks.

Most psychologists and psychiatrists now feel that this syndrome is largely due to the personality of the individual. The person was already predisposed to hallucinations; the alcohol merely precipitates them.

Coleman reported the following case to illustrate this condition:

The patient was hospitalized after a suidical attempt in which he slashed his wrists. He had been hospitalized once before after a similar incident in which he tried to hang himself with a bath towel. He was unmarried and lived alone.

The patient had been drinking excessively for a three-year period. He was not in the least particular about what he drank as long as it contained alcohol. For several days prior to his last suicidal attempt he had heard voices which accused him of all manner of "filthy sex acts." He was particularly outraged when they accused him of having committed homosexual acts with his mouth and of having had relations with animals. He complained of a terrible taste in his mouth and imagined that his food had been poisoned as a means of punishing him for his sins. He was generally fearful and apprehensive and slept poorly.

After a stay of two weeks in the hospital, the patient made a good recovery and was discharged. At this time he seemed to have some insight into his difficulties, stating that he felt that his sexual problems had something to do with suicidal attempt. (James C. Coleman, *Abnormal Psychology and Modern Life*, 3rd ed. Chicago: Scott, Foresman & Co., 1964. p. 425.)

Korsakoff's Syndrome is a group of related symptoms which was first reported by a Russian neurologist, Syergey Syervervich Korsakoff (1854-1900) in 1887. The major symptom of this condition is loss of memory, especially loss of memory for recent events. The gaps in recall are filled in by the patient with all sorts of fantastic tales. In fact, the stories often take on the characteristics of hallucinations and delusions. Paranoid delusions of persecution are common. This lack of immediate recall can lead not only to gross fabrications but to an inability to recognize even familiar objects in the immediate environment.

The most pronounced physical symptom is polyneuritis, which can lead to a wasting away of the muscles, paralysis, and extreme pain in the area of the inflamed peripheral nerves.

This condition usually occurs in older alcoholics after many years of drinking. Quite often, the patient has shown other symptoms, such as extreme suspicion, a general lowering of morals and ethics, hallucinations, and a tendency to live in the past, long before the Korsakoff pattern emerges. In addition, other types of psychotic behavior may accompany the basic syndrome.

The following case illustrates this condition:

> The patient, a 65-year-old female, had been drinking almost nightly for over 40 years. She and an alcoholic daughter escorted her 15-year-old granddaughter to the NCO club at a local army base almost every night. The night was filled with many rounds of drinks, much merriment and revelry with the soldiers. The granddaughter lived with the patient because of

several aggressive episodes while under the influence of alcohol on the part of the mother.

During this period, the granddaughter met and fell in love with a soldier. The soldier was to be discharged in about six months and had some leave time remaining. He invited the young girl to spend a week at the beach with him. The mother was invited along as a chaperon. The three went and enjoyed the week immensely.

Upon returning from the beach, the three found the patient in a jealous rage. She accused her granddaughter of being a prostitute. She accused her daughter of encouraging promiscuity. She threatened to have the soldier arrested for statutory rape. The young girl tried to mediate between her elders but to no avail. After weeks of accusations and counter-accusations the granddaughter moved back in with her mother.

The patient began to consume huge amounts of alcohol every night. She brought her bottle along with her as she stood outside in the dark to spy on her daughter and granddaughter. She convinced her daughter's husband (who at the moment was not living with his wife) that they had established a house of prostitution. Finally, they could stand the pressure no no longer, so they moved to another city.

For about two years after this, the patient stayed drunk night and day. She stayed in her house almost constantly and drank herself into unconciousness every night. When she did visit with relatives, her topic of conversation was always about how she had been persecuted and what no-good tramps her daughter and granddaughter were.

Upon hospitalization, she could not remember who she was or where she was. She appeared to be experiencing both visual and auditory hallucinations. The least noise or a stranger entering the room sent her into stark panic. She told one tale after another about her recent sexual episodes. She could not recognize her nurse if the nurse left the room for only a few minutes. She reported a tingling sensation and pain in her feet and hands.

As is usual, treatment for this patient consisted of large doses of vitamin B. No attempt at psychotherapy was made. The patient was released from the hospital in three weeks at which time she seemed to be rational and essentially free of manifest anxiety. Her daughter and granddaughter were informed of her condition. They came in to the hospital and invited her to live with them. She accepted and seemed pleased to be a member of the family once more. For about two years she functioned adequately and even found constructive work as a practical nurse. The last report on this patient was that she was back on the bottle and was beginning to sneak "nips" on a more frequent basis. She was hiding her source and denying any drinking at all.

Alcoholic dementia is a term not often used today, but when used, refers to a lack of recovery from Korsakoff's syndrome. As one would suspect, the individual maintains the memory loss, the Korsakoff condition, and there is usually intellectual impairment. As with most psychotics, the person is usually slovenly in dress and manners. He cares little about personal cleanliness and has poor judgment in moral and ethical matters. If married, the person is apt to manifest "alcoholic jealousy," that is, he is likely to accuse his mate of "running around" or some other type of "goings on," often of a sexual nature.

Treatment of alcoholism

It is thought that the causes for alcoholism are largely psychological. Psychotherapy for alcoholics has been notably unsuccessful. Many individuals go on the "water wagon" for weeks, months, or even years, but if they ever take a drink, they immediately revert to their old habits. One drink and alcohol beings to control them once more. In other words, symptoms may be arrested but the basic problem has not been resolved.

One approach to symptom arrest has had encouraging results. This is the approach of Alcoholics Anonymous. Essentially, the idea is for members to encourage one another to stay away from alcoholic beverages. The meetings are partly social and partly therapeutic. During the meeting, someone will give a testimonial about his drinking and then the balance of the time is spent in socializing. If a member is involved in a situation where his desire for alcohol is increased, he may call another member to come stay with him and help him overcome the craving. Or, if he backslides, he may call a "brother" to help him home and nurse him through the bad time.

AA has strong religious overtones. A belief in a more powerful being is required, but no effort is made to encourage any specific dogma. One of the major reasons for the success of Alcoholics Anonymous is probably the emphasis on spiritual values. Most alcoholics, in the later stages, turn to religion. Some even become religious fanatics. The appeal of AA is that it touches on something already of deep interest to the individual.

Another likely reason for the success of AA is that the alcoholic feels that, at last, he has found someone who understands. Usually he has received thousands of sermons and exhortations from people that he feels cannot possibly understand him because they have never had the experience themselves.

Currently, much research is being done employing aversive conditioning techniques in the treatment of alcoholics. Emetic drugs have been administered so that every time the person takes a drink, he will vomit. This procedure has been successful but it has one major disadvantage; many medicines contain alcohol. If emetic drugs are given the patient, he may be unable to take a large variety of medicines that could be necessary.

A more promising approach seems to be in the use of shock. The association between pain and drinking alcoholic beverages can be conditioned but the therapist should positively reinforce some substitute beverages.

To date, there have been few reports of symptom relapse or symptom substitution. However, one must bear in mind that many alcoholics have remained on the "water wagon" for years.

The real solution to the problem of alcoholism seems to lie in prevention. The following twenty questions were taken from a report by Johns Hopkins University. If you answer yes to five or more of these questions, you are a present or prospective alcoholic and should seek professional help at once.

Test for Alcoholism

1. Has your drinking harmed your home life?
2. Has your drinking harmed your sex life with your spouse?
3. Has your drinking harmed your ability to provide for your family?
4. Has your drinking caused you to be absent from work?
5. Have you ever lost a job due to drinking?
6. Have you lost status in your family role due to drinking?
7. Have you noticed that you drink more than friends at social gatherings?
8. Have you ever had blackouts or periods which you could not remember when you were drinking?
9. Do you need a drink to get up in the morning?
10. Do you feel the need to drink before you face social situations?
11. Do you drink to forget about problems?
12. Do you drink when you are alone?
13. Have you ever been arrested for drunkenness?
14. Have you ever had an automobile accident due to drinking?
15. Have you ever passed out due to drinking?
16. Have you ever had hallucinations while drinking?
17. Has your drinking ever caused you to get into fights?
18. Have your friends or relatives ever told you that you drink too much?
19. Have you ever been asked to leave a particular place due to excessive drinking?
20. Do you drink early in the day?

DRUG ADDICTION

Many physicians say that if drug addiction were not so expensive, it would be better to be addicted to some drugs than to alcohol. Whereas alcohol is a depressant, many drugs are stimulants. The person can function better in society under the mood-elevators than under the influence of alcohol. Indeed, many drugs are dangerous, but some seem to have only minor effects. However, most narcotics are treated the same by law enforcement officials, so the individual who experiments with them is taking a chance on spending some time in prison.

Just how many drug addicts there are in the United States is difficult to determine but there is no doubt that the amount of experimentation with narcotics is on the rise, especially among young people. Religious and social cults are being built around the use of certain drugs. "Psychedelic experiences," "trips," "hallucinogenics," "pot," and other terms related to drug experiences have become increasingly familiar in recent years.

At one time, about the only popular drug that could be found on a college campus was some type of amphetamine, such as benzedrine or dexadrine, the so-called pep pills. Today, almost any variety of narcotic can be purchased at most universities if you know the right people.

Not too many years ago, drug addiction was associated with being down and out. In *Brave New World,* Huxley (1932) described a society of the future in which a panacea drug, soma, would be given to everyone to keep him from experiencing anxiety. Huxley's "a gram is better than a damn" society is not too far off.

Addiction, in contrast to habituation, involves a

physiological as well as psychological dependence upon a drug. Apparently, in true addiction the narcotic becomes structurally a part of the body. The following makes the distinction between the two terms:

> Addiction is characterized by *(a)* an overpowering desire to continue taking the drug, *(b)* a tendency to increase the dosage, *(c)* psychological and physiological dependence on the drug, *(d)* detrimental effects to both the individual and society. In the case of habituation, however, *(a)* there is a desire but not a compulsion to continue taking the drug, *(b)* there is little tendency to increase the dosage, *(c)* there is some psychological but no physiological dependence, *(d)* any detrimental consequences affect the individual primarily. (M. H. Seevers, "Medical Perspectives on Habituation and Addiction," *Journal of the American Medical Association,* vol. 181, 1962, pp. 92-8.)

One of the major distinctions is that in addiction the user develops a tolerance for the drug, that is, he requires larger and larger dosages to achieve the same effects. If he is suddenly taken off the drug he will show withdrawal symptoms, a condition resembling somewhat the delirium tremens of the alcoholic. If the drug is administered during this state, the person's composure and equilibrium are usually restored in a few minutes. If the person is kept off the drug, his symptoms last, and increase in severity, for hours or days. He refuses to eat. The lack of food combined with dehydration cause severe loss of weight. Heart failure, resulting in death, is not uncommon.

There are two federal hospitals for treatment of drug addicts in the United States. These hospitals are located near Fort Worth, Texas, and Lexington, Kentucky. Most of the studies done in these centers show a recidivism rate of ninety per cent or better. In other words, almost all addicts are back for treatment within a short period of time. Apparently, drug addicts commit themselves for therapy so that they can start over with a much smaller dosage. This is especially true of the users of opium and its derivatives.

In discussing drugs, one must try to make a distinction between the effects of the drugs. Some stimulate, like cocaine and the amphetamines (benzedrine and dexadrine); and others narcotize, like opiates and barbiturates. For years, the narcotizing drugs were considered to be the only truly addictive drugs. This was based largely on the assumption that increasing tolerance is the major signal of physiological dependence. If one uses the criterion of detrimental effects to both the individual and society, as the World Health Organization does, then several other drugs, cocaine, for example, would have to be classified as addictive.

Opiates

Opium and some of its more powerful derivatives, notably morphine and heroin, are the most powerful drugs known to man. Their addictive properties are beyond doubt. Opium is usually introduced into the body by smoking. This substance, derived from the seed of the Oriental poppy, has been around about as long as there has been a recorded history of man. Typically the beginning user of morphine or heroin starts out by sniffing the drug into his nose. Later he wants faster effects, so he injects the substance directly into his bloodstream by using a hypodermic syringe. This use of a syringe is called main lining.

The early effects of the opiates are euphoria, a feeling of dreamlike floating and contentment, immunity to pain, and little contact with stimuli from the environment. The person is totally relaxed and "all is right with the world." This attitude of, "Like man, it ain't no big thing. Don't sweat the small stuff," lasts for a few hours, and then the individual starts to drop. He becomes more and more depressed, begins to have discomfort in his stomach, becomes weary in mind and body, and feels oppressed. The letdown leads to a desire to "go up" again. Because the person is "low," it takes a larger dosage to get back as "high" as he was previously. If he does not allow the depression to work itself off, he can become addicted in a short period of time.

Most morphine or heroin addicts soon begin to look and feel unhealthy. The complexion takes on a sickly, yellowish hue. They seem to age rapidly. There is a general loss of interest in everything except their habit. Social and personal involvements are hindered or severed, except with other users. They complain of the "jitters" or the "shakes." Even their movement pattern changes; they now slink around as though they were hiding from everyone. Usually, the general weakness is accompanied by loss of appetite, so that an "asthenic vicious circle" is set into motion.

Since most opiates have to be obtained on the black market in the United States, they are quite expensive. As the individuals' tolerance for the drugs grows, more and more money is required to support the habit. Most people cannot earn enough in a legitimate way to pay for the drug after they have become addicted. So, they are forced into the fringe world of crime to earn the required amount of money.

There are more female opiate addicts than male. If the "junky" is a woman, she will probably turn to prostitution. This pattern is probably responsible for the popular misconception that all drugs are aphrodisiacs, or sex stimulants. In actuality, the opiates decrease sexual desire.

If the addict is a man, he may become a "pusher," that is, he may try to induce others into his dream world. This often is done by giving a young person his first experience. Then, later, as the youth becomes "hooked," he is charged for the "fix." On the other hand, the underworld is not too interested in the "junky pusher." He is not very dependable. Consequently, most "dope peddlers" are not addicts themselves. The result is that the male addict is often forced into other illegal or semi-legal activities. He may beg, borrow, or steal to obtain the necessary loot.

There is usually a lowering of moral and ethical restraints in any type of addiction, but not all of this can be attributed to the physical properties of the drug itself. A part of the blame must be directed to the social and cultural mores. In countries such as England where drug addiction is not illegal, the consequences of the habit are often less severe. In this situation, the cost of the drug is kept at a reasonable level, the addicts are not forced into a life of crime or prostitution. The real criminals are the pushers and syndicate mobsters. Morphine and heroin addicts, in their euphoric state, are too happy and carefree to commit voilent crimes.

Correspondingly, there is little or no evidence to suggest that the chemical properties of the opiates have any direct detrimental effects on the bodies of the users. Most addicts decline in physical health after prolonged usage, but this is probably due to improper diet, overexposure to the elements, and lack of interest in physical hygiene. Also, an overdose of any drug can have toxic effects.

Two derivatives of opium which are not often mentioned are paregoric and codeine. Paregoric, of course, is the medicine we give our babies to put them to sleep or to reduce stomach discomforts. Two of the principal ingredients in this compound are alcohol and morphine sulfate. Codeine is widely used in cough syrups. Both have been largely brought under legislative control but it is still possible to obtain paregoric without a prescription in some states. Codeine and paregoric addiction are not often reported but there are probably many cases in the United States. The following illustrates the point:

> The patient, a 45-year-old male, was hospitalized because of paregoric addiction. His consumption had reached about three pints per week. His addiction was discovered when he was jailed for acting "strangely." He pleaded over and over for some paregoric. An alcoholic rehabilitation man was called in by the local police officials because they did not know what to do or what was happening. The caseworker went out, bought a small bottle of paregoric, and gave it to the patient. The subject soon regained his composure after gulping down the paregoric.
>
> The rehabilitation man then discovered that the patient had been consuming large amounts of paregoric for years. He would go from one drug store to another obtaining small bottles of the substance. He had never been reported by a pharmacist because he spread the purchases over such a wide area that no one became suspicious. In his home state, small amounts of paregoric could be sold without a doctor's prescription. Druggists were required to report those cases where the volume of purchases seemed unreasonable.
>
> The caseworker had great difficulty in getting his patient committed to Lexington because of reluctance on the part of the court to sign the necessary papers. After much time and effort, commitment was obtained.

In summary, the opiates are strongly addictive drugs. Once a person has become addicted, the chances of recovery are almost nil. Regardless of whether the habit began with morphine as a pain killer in a hospital or whether the individual actively experimented for "kicks," the outcome is the same—a hopeless, helpless, pathetic shell of humanity. These are not "mind expanding" drugs; they are cripplers. The addict is not a criminal; he needs help.

A hopeful new approach to treatment of drug addicts has now been started. This organization, Synanon (Coleman, 1964) is partly patterned after Alcoholics Anonymous and partly patterned after halfway houses. The first Synanon House was established in 1958, in Santa Monica, California. The founder of this movement was Charles E. Dederick, a dynamic individual who had at one time been an alcoholic. He began the movement with alcoholics but later included ex-criminal drug addicts.

In the Synanon House members learn social roles, serve as therapists for one another, and serve to help reduce stress and anxiety in newcomers. Gradually, they are encouraged to move out of the sheltered community into the community-at-large. As in AA, many members make Synanon their life work.

In his book, *Reality Therapy: A New Approach to Psychiatry,* William Glasser (1965) pointed out that, for most Americans, there are two basic needs which are exceptionally difficult to fulfill, the need to feel worthwhile and the need to love and be loved. Glasser divided behavior into only two categories, responsible or irresponsible. Certainly the addict of any type is manifesting irresponsible behavior. Synanon seems to have unlimited potential for satisfying the two basic needs and for changing the ex-criminal addict's behavior into socially and personally responsible behavior.

Barbiturates

Chemically, the barbiturates are derivatives of barbituric acid, a crystalline powder which has sedative and hypnotic properties. These compounds are widely employed in sleeping pills, the most common form being phenobarbital. This group of drugs is considered truly addictive in the sense that the individual builds up a tolerance. Larger and larger doses are required to obtain the same effects. On the other hand, many people are able to keep intake under control because, apparently, there is not the intense craving that is reported with other drugs.

As is well known, the taking of an overdose of sleeping pills is one of the more popular modes of committing suicide in America. Many accidental deaths can be traced to a combination of alcohol and barbiturates. Since both are central nervous system depressants, the combined effect can slow the vital functions to the point of fatality.

In common usage, the effect of these drugs is a slowing down of cortical processes. This, in turn, leads to a general slowing down and drowsiness. The person's thinking becomes hazy and somewhat disoriented. Nyswander (1959) considered a person who takes three or more sleeping pills a night a likely candidate for barbiturate addiction. However, there are many people who maintain this level of consumption without showing signs of chronic poisoning. Barbiturate addicts are more likely to kill themselves outright than they are to end up in a hospital.

In acute poisoning the syndrome is usually a dry mouth and throat with difficulty in swallowing, a decreased ability to taste and smell, digestive and gastric discomfort, and, if the person tries to walk, a staggering and reeling gait. If the dose is large enough, the person will die, usually of cardiac collapse.

Chronic poisoning is marked by general slowing down in mental, emotional, and physical processes. Disorientation, memory distortion, and hazy thinking are typical. Making a choice may become almost impossible.

Where there has been prolonged and excessive use of these drugs, the probability of brain injury is high. This can lead to other complicating symptoms of a prepsychotic or psychotic nature. If the person does end up in a hospital, his withdrawal symptoms are generally considered to be more severe than those of morphine and heroin addicts. (Osnos, 1963).

Barbiturates are controlled fairly tightly at present. It is difficult to obtain these drugs without the prescription of a doctor. The black market is generally not as interested in this type of narcotic as it is in the opiates and other drugs. In addition, hundreds of non-prescription sleeping pills which contain no barbiturates may be obtained at any pharmacy.

Amphetamines

There are a large number of these drugs on the market but the principal two are benzedrine and dexadrine. Benzedrine, at one time, was a popular ingredient in nasal inhalers. Since this drug has been brought under tight narcotics control, other substances have largely replaced it in these inhalers. A second usage of benzedrine is based upon its anti-fatigue producing qualities. These attributes have led to the introduction of the drug in tablet form and explain why it is often called a pep pill. College students, especially during final examinations, and truck drivers have used this drug for decades to stay awake.

When it becomes increasingly difficult to obtain benzedrine, people who want to be "pepped up" turn to a more easily obtainable amphetamine, dexadrine. This drug is the base for many diet pills. It is easy to obtain without a prescription because so many people are on diets, also many pharmacists will oblige a friend because dexadrine is considered much less dangerous than benzedrine.

Young people, seeking "kicks", often combine amphetamines with alcoholic beverages, the result of which used to be called a benny. The depressant effects of alcohol and the stimulating properties of benzedrine can lead to some bizarre consequences. Some shocking and and weird crimes have been committed by individuals under the influence of both of these agents. On the other hand, most people feel nervous and jumpy and report tremors while under the influence of amphetamines. A small amount of alcohol can take the edge off these "shakes."

Amphetamines are powerful cortical stimulants. The effects are generally those of euphoria. The person feels wide awake, contented, self-assured, and talkative. He feels that no problem is too big for him to tackle. A college student can stay awake all night studying for exams and, if he takes another pill in the morning before the examination, approach the situation with total confidence. There is some question as to whether the student does learn better under the influence of these drugs because of decreased anxiety, or whether he merely thinks he learns better. Certainly, decreased anxiety could produce a situation more conducive to learning.

The effects of benzedrine usually last from four to six hours. In the later stage, the individual begins to feel sleepy, drowsy, and generally depressed. It is during this depressed stage that habituation may occur. If the person uses additional drugs to lift him up again, he may require larger doses to reach the previous "high." If an addictive personality, that is, a person with strong desires to escape reality, is involved, a psychological dependency may develop rapidly. After all, the feelings under the influence of amphetamines are usually happy, pleasant experiences. Big problems become small; small problems are like the old soldier — "they just fade away."

Hallucinations can develop if the person stays awake long enough continually replenishing the drug. These false perceptions are usually visual. The following is an illustration:

> The young couple had been driving continually for more than 40 hours. Every four or five hours they had stopped for a cup of coffee and a benzedrine tablet. The husband turned to his wife and said, "Did you see that?" She grinned and said, "I saw it, but I don't believe it — a zebra walking down the middle of the highway." "But I saw an elephant, not a zebra," he said. "Look over there, why, it's an entire circus."

As can be seen, the "pink elephant" misconception of alcoholic hallucinations applies more to amphetamine intoxication than it does to psychoses related to alcoholism. The couple in the above example began to hallucinate at approximately the same time. Both "saw" large animals and large moving objects, not the insects or small creatures of the alcoholic hallucination.

Cocaine

For centuries, the Indians in the high plateau country of South America have been observed chewing on the leaves of the cacao (or coca) plant. Their long endurance plus their appearance of being narcotized led to the discovery of a large number of narcotics which can be derived from this plant, the most notable of which is cocaine. Cocaine is a powerful cortical stimulant which produces an euphoric state in the user. The symptoms are the typical euphoric symptoms, such as contentment, extreme confidence, talkativeness, and exhilaration. In addition, cocaine produces some effects which differ from the opiates, namely, wakefulness, excitement, and some sexual stimulation. However, most users report a period of dizziness and headaches (Coleman, 1964) preceding the euphoric state.

"Trip" has become a household word in the United States. Of all drugs, cocaine is the most likely to produce a "bad trip," a state in which the person sees, hears, or feels frightening and terrifying things. For this reason, many addicts are afraid of this drug. The "cocaine bug" can lead to permanent psychosis. The chronic addict (addiction may be misused here because there is little evidence to suggest physiological dependence) usually shows extreme depression, pallor, weakness, and digestive upsets. Hallucinations and paranoid delusions are not uncommon.

As with most narcotics, cocaine generally leads to moral and ethical deterioration after prolonged usage. Sexual perversions are associated quite often with cocaine addiction. The drug becomes the center of the person's life. He becomes preoccupied with ways and means of obtaining an additional supply. All other values are secondary to the habit. Friends and relatives are either used or abandoned. Nothing is important except the drug itself.

Peyote and Mescaline

Most of the Indians of North America have a long tradition of the prophetic value of the vision. Occupations, status, and mates were determined by dreams and visions. The males, in many tribes, when they reached a certain age, were sent out on a "vision quest." They would do almost anything—starve themselves, overexpose themselves to the elements, go without sleep for days on end—in order to have their "vision." It is little wonder, then, that the Indians of the southwest United States were the first to discover one of the most powerful of the hallucinogenic drugs, peyote.

Peyote is the top portion of the mescale cactus, a plant which grows largely under ground. The portion above ground is cut off and is sold as a "peyote button." The "button" contains seven alkaloids, any one of which could become a separate narcotic if extracted. Mescaline is the most noted of the derivatives of peyote.

"Peyotism" has spread from the southwest to almost every Indian tribe in North America. It is, by far, the most popular religion among the Indians. The drug is used in the religious ceremonies to induce visions. Almost everyone who has taken peyote reports vivid and colorful visual hallucinations. Among the Indians, these hallucinations are usually pleasant, and because of the background and setting, are of a religious nature. In addition, peyote seems to be a sexual stimulant; so many of the ceremonies terminate in an orgy. Peyotism is legal in the United States for Indians, but not for anyone else.

Because of the aphrodisiac and hallucinogenic properties of peyote, many young non-Indian thrill-seekers have been attracted to the use of the drug. However, there appears to be one major difference between Indian cultures and the major American culture which makes peyote an extremely dangerous drug when taken by the non-Indian. Many senseless and violent crimes in which the victim was not only killed, but brutally and viciously mutilated, have been reported when this drug was used by persons other than Indians. Apparently, peyote has properties that can release repressed hostility in a very explosive manner. And, of course, repressed hostility is a major problem in American society.

Mescaline has several effects similar to those of peyote and some effects which are different. As with peyote, mescaline produces vivid halucinations, usually in technicolor. Under the influences, the user may sit and stare at a flower, a flame, or a painting for hours. Minute details may form a configuration of metaphysical beauty, or the patterns may float in and out. Time, distance, and objects may become distorted or more clearly focused. Details that were once in the background may stand out as the figure. Perceptual distortion or hypersensitivity may expand from vision to other senses. Unlike peyote, mescaline seems to have a soothing effect on the person. Euphoric indifference is often reported. The will to fight for anything seems to disappear.

Aldous Huxley became interested in mescaline when he first heard about it. He thought this drug might be the *soma* of his *Brave New World* (1943). As a result, he decided to try this drug for himself. Two books, *The Doors of Perception* (1963) and *Heaven and Hell* (1963) were written about his experiences while under the influence of mescaline. Huxley concluded that mescaline is not soma but that it is not far away from the "gram is better than a damn" drug.

LSD (lysergic acid diethylamide)

Several years ago, flower seed distributors had a run on morning glory seeds. It was discovered that many people were consuming these seeds and receiving narcotic effects. This led to the discovery of LSD, a chemical compound which was easy to synthesize. The synthesized version could be taken in much larger doses and some rather startling effects could be achieved. The early users of LSD ushered in a new era in concepts and information about drug addiction.

Before LSD, drug addiction was associated with being

down and out, having no will power and a weak moral character. The first users of LSD were, in large measure, professional people. Many were associated with universities and they were conducting experiments on themselves as well as others. New words and phrases, such as hallucinogenic, psychedelic, psychotomimetic, and mind-expansion began to become commonplace. These people got together on weekends for parties but functioned normally during the week. They showed no signs of moral and ethical decay. They could not be identified as addictive personalities nor could they be accused of antisocial acts. They were a new breed of drug users. They were conducting legitimate experiments on schizophrenia or they were seeking "mind-expansion" or a "spiritual rebirth."

Then, a group of Harvard professors, the most notable of whom was Timothy Leary, was fired for its experiments with LSD. Leary and his group went to Mexico and a new religious cult was born. Essentially, "peyotism" was the model. If the Indians could have a religion based on the use of a drug, then why not other Americans they argued. The International Federation for Internal Freedom (IFIF) was established in 1963 in Zihutanejo, Mexico. This was to be an experiment in "transpersonative" (a word coined by Alan Watts, the expert on Zen Buddhism) living. This term referred to: "Increased perceptivity, reduced defensiveness, heightened insight, enhanced interpersonal sensitivity, and acceptance . . ." (Downing, Chapter VIII in Blum et al., 1964). The Mexican authorities did not tolerate this type of experiment so the group moved back to New York state. A great deal of publicity was received during the hassle between the IFIF group and the governmental authorities.

The initials LSD became a household word. "Acid,"

"pearly gates," "heavenly blue," "royal blue," and "wedding bells" began to take on new meaning in the language. People out for kicks found that the "sugar cube" was one of the most powerful ways to "tune in, turn on, and drop out." The hallucinogenic and euphoric properties of LSD were, at first, exalted. The use of this drug was supposed to be a way to expand the mind.

Later, the negative aspects of LSD began to be reported. "Bad trips," psychotic episodes, and flashbacks were associated with usage of the drug. A few experiments indicated the possibility of chromosomal damage. Other studies implied a chance that there might be permanent changes in certain structures of the brain after habitual usage. Many people, even some "heads," were frightened away from LSD and switched to marijuana, a compound with less firmly established side effects.

Marijuana and Hashish

Marijuana is derived from the cannabis plant, a weed that will grow almost anywhere under extremely varied conditions. It is the North American version of hashish which has been widely used in the Orient and Near East for centuries.

In Chapter XII of *Utopiates,* Blum and Wahl presented the typical police views on the alcohol-marijuana dilemma.

a) Both are intoxicating, but marijuana creates criminal tendencies.

b) Unlike alcohol, marijuana use, itself not dangerous, leads to the use of heroin.

c) Both the drunk and the marijuana user are befuddled by intoxication and may lose the capacity to distinguish right from wrong. But the drunk is made helpless and incapable of action by alcohol, whereas the marijuana user remains physically able and, further, may be impelled to criminal acts by stimulation of the drug.

d) Alcohol has a number of benign effects; it tastes good, it stimulates the appetite, it facilitates social interactions so that it is pleasant to take as well as being capable, in moderate use, of producing pleasant results. Marijuana has no such inherently benign characteristics; it is not pleasurable *in itself,* but can be used only to achieve an end state for which the means, smoking "pot," is merely instrumental.

e) There is no difference except the social facts; alcohol is acceptable and legal; marijuana use is rejected by those who set social standards, and it is illegal.

f) Different types of persons choose to use marijuana and alcohol; primarily those with psychopathic or antisocial trends select marijuana.

g) The use of marijuana necessarily puts the user in association with persons operating illegally, for he depends upon them for a source of supply. Consequently, the user is exposed to a group which is likely to be immoral or unethical, and he runs the risk of adopting their dishonesty and bad habits. This exposes him to a criminal career just because of his marijuana habit.

h) Marijuana use is associated with unpredictability of behavior, whereas alcohol use leads to predictable behavior. The marijuana user himself may not know how he will respond to the next stick; the alcohol user knows quite well what a drink will do. Furthermore, those who live or deal with the marijuana user not only are faced with uncertainty as to what he will do, but they have no way of knowing that he is under the influence of a drug. The alcohol user, either by smell or action, is clearly identified as being under its influence, and the persons with him can anticipate what he will do and can adjust their actions to their predictions. The marijuana user on a "high" cannot be identified by those around him (unless he tells them or has taken it with them), and so they are unprepared for irrational or reckless behavior and can do nothing to protect themselves or even the user.

i) Alcohol is worse than marijuana by any measure of pharmacological effect. It produces more bizarre behavior, it produces more physical damage, it produces hangover, and so on.

j) Both alcohol and marijuana are potentially dangerous and addictive; neither necessarily so. Social and personality factors must be considered in anticipating effects. (Richard Blum et al. *Utopiates*. New York: Atherton Press, 1964, pp. 227-9.)

The youth of America, in ever increasing numbers, are rejecting these attitudes with the exception of assumptions (e) and (i). As Paul Harvey, the conservative radio and television commentator, pointed out on WSOC-TV, Charlotte, North Carolina, on October 3, 1969, a revolution is on our hands. Young people are saying, "Look man, you take your sleeping pills at night, a pep pill to get started on in the morning, several 'snorts' during the day, and you accuse us of being 'potheads.' You may be selling, but we are not buying." Youth wants some evidence, not just dogmatic opinions. And the authorities are far from agreement on the effects of marijuana usage, much less the social consequences.

About all that can be said regarding the effects of marijuana at the present is that it is psychedelic, that is, it does alter the mind. Perceptual distortion or changes are frequently reported. Near objects may appear far away or vice versa. Even here, there seems to be some control over the situation; an object may be made to approach or it may be made to recede. Minute details may take on fascinating qualities. Time perspective can become grossly or slightly changed. A minute may seem like an hour or a lifetime may rush by the viewer in a few seconds.

Little has been done empirically to determine the effects of prolonged usage of marijuana. There is a small amount of evidence that prolonged usage (five years or more) does produce some cerebral deterioration, as shown in memory and speech disturbances, disorientation, and poor judgment. There studies were conducted in Morocco with a sample of habitual hashish users. (Masserman, 1967).

In conclusion, the 1950s have been described as the decade in which we discovered atomic power; the 1960s gave us "youth power." (NBC special, *Into the Seventies,* October 7, 1969). This "youth power" is going to be with us for some time to come and marijuana smoking has become a social issue that demands some conclusive empirical evidence.

Bromide and salicylic compounds

Bromide compounds and salicylic compounds are so common that few people think of them as potentially dangerous drugs. These common patent drugs are sold to relieve headaches, digestive discomfort, nervous tension, colds, backaches, and cramps. Bromide compounds are usually combined with other substances such as the antipyretics (for example, phenetide) which also can become habit-forming. Both the bromides and the antipyretics have a cumulative effect, that is, they are stored more easily than they are eliminated. These pain-killing substances are taken daily by large numbers of people in doses that can be and often are dangerous. Bromide poisoning can lead to tremors and delirium, a state resembling delirium tremors in the alcoholic. If the person continues to take his pain-killer, death is probable.

The salicyclic compounds (notably aspirin) can also become habit-forming. Aspirin, like the bromides, is used mostly to kill pain, reduce fever, or induce sleep. Few people realize that these compounds are as dangerous as they really are. Many mothers give their children aspirin every night to help them go to sleep. Of course, everyone has heard of the hundreds of babies that have been killed by overdoses of baby aspirin, but few people realize that there are adult "addicts" to the salicylic compounds. Quite often, these "addicts" are also "addicted" to a soft drink. When they take their powder or tablet, they also drink a cola. Delirium, unconsciousness, mental deterioration, and other physical symptoms may be induced by an overdose of these drugs or by prolonged abuse.

In the mountain regions of Appalachia, the old-timers refer to certain soft drinks as "dope." Of course, the author does not know the formula of these beverages, but there does seem to be a strong tendency for some people to become habituated. At least one of the better-known colas originally entered the market as a patented medicine.

5
psychoses

Since this book is for the beginner in psychology, not a great deal of detail will be included in this chapter. In the psychotic reactions, there is severe personality disturbance, extreme disorientation in thought and behavior, blunting or exaggeration of emotions, and a general withdrawal pattern. Therefore, most psychotics are placed in mental institutions.

In popular language, the word insanity is often applied to psychotic behavior. However, the term insanity is a legal term and has no psychological or medical meaning. It simply means that the person is not legally responsible for his actions. Several mental states other than psychosis can be so defined in the courts.

This chapter will be concerned with the so-called functional psychoses. Psychotic behavior with well defined organic causation will not be discussed. Organic psychosis is a medical problem and will not be discussed in this book. The functional psychoses are a group of behavior patterns with no clear-cut organic basis. These conditions usually are classified into one of the following categories: (1) schizophrenic reactions, (2) paranoid reactions, (3) affective reactions, and (4) involutional psychotic reactions.

In most psychotic episodes, one or more of the following usually occur: (1) hallucinations, (2) delusions, and (3) stereotypes. In the following discussion, the word illusion is included because of its close relationship to the hallucination.

Illusion is a false sensory impression which has some basis in reality. For example, a person may be driving down a highway and "see" water ahead. When he reaches the point where the water appeared, there is no water. The ever-popular mirage of the desert is another example. Illusions can be explained on the basis of some natural phenomenon and have been dealt with adequately by the perceptual psychologists.

Hallucinations, like illusions, are false sensory impressions, but unlike illusions, there are no natural or scientific explanations for them. Whereas illusions can be shared with other people, hallucinations are private and personal. No one else can hear the voices or see the "visions."

Hallucinations may involve any of the senses. In alcoholism and drug addiction, visual misperceptions are the type most frequently reported. In the functional psychoses, auditory hallucinations are by far the most common. Voices, clanging chains, motors, electrical static, and ringing telephones are heard. For example, one patient kept hearing a telephone ringing in his stomach. He had been a telephone linesman before admittance into a mental hospital.

The voices of the psychotic most often center on sexual and/or aggressive themes. Usually, the patient hears horrible, vulgar, dirty, sinful words being spoken. As a rule, the voices center around impulses which the person himself finds unacceptable, for example, sexual perversion, homicide, and suicide. Or if the individual also has delusions, the voices will probably include components of the delusion; for instance, if paranoid delusions are in evidence, the patient may hear voices talking about communist plots or FBI conspiracies against him.

Haptic (touch), olfactory (smell), and gustatory (taste) hallucinations are not as common as visual and auditory misperceptions but they do occur. For example, the patient may feel bugs crawling around over his body, smell poison gas, or taste arsenic in his coffee. Sometimes, a person will experience a number of different hallucinations. This is especially true when the individual is in a delirious state.

Delusions are dogmatic beliefs which are contrary to fact. Most individuals with delusions will refuse to change their opinions regardless of how much evidence to the contrary is presented. A delusion may be highly systematic as in the "communist plot" opinion expressed in several current books on politics, or the delusion may be disorganized, bizarre, and totally unbelievable, such as a paranoid delusion in which the person thinks he is Christ or Napoleon.

Delusions may center around any topic, but the following are the most common:

1. *Delusions of sin and guilt*—a belief that the individual has committed some horrible and unforgivable sin, e.g. that he, and he alone, was responsible for World War II. Usually the patient thinks that his actions have harmed unlimited numbers of people. Some suicides have been precipitated by this type of delusion. As one patient expressed it, "Everything I touch turns to feces (not his term) and everyone I get involved with gets hurt by me. I must die for my sins."

2. *Hypochondriacal delusions*—the opinion that one's health is malignant or that he has a disease which physicians have never heard of. Included here are such beliefs as "my guts

have turned to sawdust," "I have a colony of ants between my skull and the skin covering it." Rot, decay, stench, and water in the bloodstream are often mentioned.

3. *Nihilistic delusions* — the false belief that the person, himself, does not exist or that nothing whatsoever exists. The following joke illustrates the point: The patient believed himself to be dead, so his psychiatrist told him to repeat over and over to himself, "Dead people don't bleed — dead people don't bleed." The patient walked around for days repeating these words. Upon his return to the psychiatrist, he was punctured in the thumb with a pin. Blood gushed forth. The psychiatrist said, "Now what do you say?" Gazing at the stream of blood, the patient said, "Hmmm — dead people do bleed." Another version of nihilistic delusion is the belief that everything and everybody is merely "Adam's dream."

4. *Delusions of persecution* — the individual feels that he is the victim of a conspiracy, that others are out to get him, that he is being plotted against. The FBI, communists, and Jews are favorites in group lots, but individuals may become the conspirers, e.g., a wife, mother-in-law, parent, offspring, neighbor, friend, etc. "Poison pen" letters have been known to set this type of delusion into motion.

5. *Delusions of reference* — the person believes that his life is the center of conversation, that, somehow, a movie or television series is about him. This type of delusion is common in small towns because there is an element of truth in the "being talked about" suspicion.

6. *Delusions of influence* — an attitude that one's mind is being altered or tampered with by some outside agency or foe. Electrical waves, ESP, and astrological influences are often mentioned as the means of obtaining these results. A favorite, in recent years, has been suspicion that fluoride or LSD placed in the water supply is being conducted in mass by the communists as a part of the communist takeover. These chemicals are supposed to alter our minds, to weaken our morals, to influence us to become communists or communist stooges.

7. *Delusions of grandeur* — with persecution, the most prevalent of all delusions. The person believes himself to be someone special, to have supernatural powers, to be a "chosen one," to be a prophet of God. Many authors and political figures have

a sense of destiny that grows out of borderline or actual delusions of grandeur. (Adapted from James C. Coleman, *Abnormal Psychology and Modern Life*, 3rd ed. Chicago: Scott, Foresman & Co., 1964, p. 265.)

The following case, diagnosed as a paranoid schizophrenic, illustrates how a combination of delusions can occur.

During an interview, the 50-year-old female patient expressed beliefs covering almost the entire range of delusions. She felt that her niece was in on a plot with other relatives (persecution) to take away the property she owned in 106 countries (grandeur) which she was planning to use, after training religious missionaries, to establish missions to convert the heathens (grandeur).

In spite of the fact that her husband was alive and visited her weekly, she maintained that her husband was dead (nihilism) and that he had been killed, beheaded, and skinned by the FBI (persecution). The FBI had six agents assigned to her alone, and had killed her husband (persecution). She had learned of their spying and talking about her (reference) from the television where they were portraying her life in several of the continuing series programs (reference). She had learned other things about the plot from the voices (auditory hallucination) that came between the television programs and the commercials. She was convinced that the hospital attendants were in on the conspiracy and that poison was being placed in her food (persecution). She was also concerned about the electrical waves that were "messing up" her mind (influence).

Stereotypy refers to any constant, repetitive act. These repeated actions are often observed in psychotic patients. The person may sit and rock back and forth, pace the floor wringing his hands, rub some part of his body continually. *Verbigeration,* or continually repeating a phrase or sentence, is another type of stereotypy. The action and the words often occur together.

Perseveration of posture, as in the rigid catatonic

state, is a third pattern. The patient may remain frozen in a given posture for hours or days. A final form of stereotypy is *perseveration of place.* One patient in a nearby mental hospital has sat in the same rocking chair rocking much of the time, for a period of over thirty years. She has huge knots on her back from the constant bouncing of her back against the chair.

Schizophrenia

The old name for this disorder was *dementia praecox,* which means a deterioration in the young. This term was unfortunate because it implied that this essentially psychological condition might be the result of nerve cell degeneration. The *praecox* portion of the phrase was equally misleading because the translation of this word is "occurring at an early age." This led many people to associate the disorder with children and adolescents, and schizophrenia rarely occurs in these age groups. It does, on the average, occur earlier than other types of psychotic breakdowns but the average age at onset of symptoms is between 25 and 35 years, depending on the type of schizophrenia which develops.

In 1911, Eugen Bleuler introduced the current term schizophrenia, which can be as misleading as the former term. Too often, people equate "the splitting of the personality" in schizophrenia with the multiple personality of the dissociative type. Bleuler did not intend to imply split personality when he used the word; instead he attempted to describe a condition in which portions of the psyche split off and take over the psychological life of the individual.

The word schizophrenia covers a hodgepodge of disorders but some or several of the following symptoms prevail: (1) association defects, (2) emotional disturbance, quite often a blunting of emotions, (3) emotional and intellectual ambivalence, (4) autism, fantasy – a tendency to withdraw into an internal world, (4) inability to stick to an activity, (7) unusual or bizarre behavior, (8) hallucination, delusions, and/or stereotypes, and (9) disturbances in moral and ethical controls.

The acute symptoms, quoted and paraphrased from the *Psychiatric Dictionary,* are:

1) Melancholia – an acute depressive state which appears to be superficial, misdirected or unreasonable – Hypochondriacal delusions are frequent.

2) Mania – the prevailing mood is capriciousness rather than euphoria or triumph, and withdrawal can usually be seen.

3) Catatonic – a frozen, statue-like stupor. Lack of contact with the environment is evident.

4) Delusional states with hallucinations, which are often visual and less stereotyped than the hallucinations seen in the chronic syndromes.

5) Twilight states – including religious ecstasies and other dream-like conditions in which desires, impulses, or fears are represented in a direct or symbolic way as being already fulfilled.

6) Benommenheit (psychic 'benumbing') – in which there is a slowing up of all psychic processes, usually in conjunction with an incapacity for dealing with any relatively complicated or unusual situation.

7) Confusion, incoherence – as a result of fragmentation of associations, speech is disconnected, sentences are half broken, and activity is excessive, purposeless, and random.

8) Anger states – with cursing, vilification, uncontrolled rage outbursts, often in relation to seemingly insignificant external events.

9) Anniversary excitements – episodes of agitation

appearing only on definite calendar days, usually related to a specific event in the patient's past.

10) Stupor.

11) Deliria—acute hallucinatory episodes often resembling the fever deliria. This condition usually occurs after a traumatic experience. The hallucinations are often accompanied by confusion, bewilderment, and narrowed consciousness.

12) Fugue states—running away in intercurrent episodes of agitation and excitement, sometimes in response to a hallucinatory command.

13) Dipsomania—tense, anxious moods drive some patients to drink heavily, until they become exhausted. *

Bleuler listed four major syndromes of schizophrenia, namely, simple, catatonic, hebephrenic, and paranoid. Several other types have been classified since Bleuler's time. For example, the American Psychiatric Association lists five additional forms: childhood, acute undifferentiated, chronic undifferentiated, schizo-affective, and residual types. Some medical people include three more forms: ambulatory, pseudoneurotic, and pseudopsychopathic schizophrenia.

Simple schizophrenia has been called the skid row disease, since the pattern of behavior can cause a person to end up on skid row because of irresponsibility, lack of contact with the environment, and a general apathy toward living.

In general, the pattern is slow in developing, with a gradual waning of interests, a general emotional indifference, a lowering of desire to indulge in social intercourse, and a steadily increasing bizarreness. Family

---

*Quoted and paraphrased from Leland E. Hinsie and Robert J. Campbell, *Psychiatric Dictionary,* 3rd ed. (New York: Oxford University Press, 1960), pp. 659-60.

and friends often mistake the condition for irresponsibility, carelessness, and lack of ambition. In the beginning, the person may show aggressive outbursts followed by seclusiveness, but eventually the isolation pattern becomes, by far, the most prevalent. Speech becomes limited. The person talks little or not at all, and when he does talk, the topic of conversation is trivial, general, or nonsensical.

The final stage is a state of asocial disinterest. By this time, most individuals have been abandoned by or have abandoned friends and relatives. The person will lead an aimless and disinterested existence. He may take an occasional job as an unskilled laborer or he may be content to beg for a meager existence. By this time, the delusions and hallucinations, which were common earlier, have largely disappeared. Fantasy life is practically nonexistent.

In contrast to most psychotics, simple schizophrenics are not often institutionalized. Instead, they live on the margin of society as vagabonds, vagrants, eccentric recluses, or if women, prostitutes. They exist from day to day, with little care about the world, the environment, or the future. On the other hand, several studies have shown simple schizophrenics who had an almost pathetic desire for contact with other people (c.f. Kant, 1948). However, this reaching out for others is often inhibited by fear.

Simple schizophrenia develops early (average age about 25) and usually shows progressive deterioration. These are unfavorable prognostic signs. The pre-psychotic personality is usually one of severe maladjustment, often with sexual and aggressive inhibitions. (Kant, 1948). If more people would recognize the warnings, the prognosis would probably become more favorable.

Catatonic schizophrenia is characterized by two catatonic reaction patterns, the suggestible and the negativistic. In both syndromes, the patient fluctuates between stupor and excitement. In the stuporous state, the person remains frozen in an immobile statue-like pose. Quite often, these postures are symbolic, for example, the fetal position or the military "at attention" pose.

In the suggestible patients, if one moves a part of the body, that part will remain in whatever position it is placed, much like the dummy in the department store window. This is called *cerea flexibilitas* or waxy flexibility. The patient may hold this posture for hours or days. Sometimes, this immobile posture is held long enough to cause swelling and blueness in the feet, ankles, and hands.

The patient shows no interest or concern with the external environment or with his internal organic processes. He will not respond to sudden stimulation, such as loud noises, nor to painful stimuli, such as a pin prick or electrical shock applied to the skin. The suggestible catatonics sometimes show *echopraxia,* a condition in which the person acts like an automaton, with a monotonous repetition of action, or *echolalia,* a mechanical repetition of certain words or phrases.

The more usual form of catatonic stupor is the negativistic variety. In this type of patient, if one tries to move a part of the body, he meets with muscular resistance. The body part springs back into its original position as soon as it is released. The patient pays no attention to his environment. Saliva may drip down his chin or he may wet or soil himself. He, like the suggestible type, will not respond to sudden or even painful stimulation. Commands or instructions bring about no response at all. However, it is a mistake to assume that the patient does not hear the people around him because several cases have been reported where a derogatory remark was made about a patient while he was immobile, and hours later he came out of his stupor, sought out the individual who made the remark, and tried to punch him in the nose.

The case of A.C., aged 32, will illustrate many of the features observed both in the excited and the stuporous phases of catatonia.

The patient's father was stubborn and self-willed, his mother was excitable and temperamental. At seven years of age he went to live with his grandparents. The grandfather, whose "word was law," suffered from epileptic seizures and subsequently died in a hospital for mental diseases; he had no understanding of the child's point of view. His seizures greatly frightened the boy. The patient was a seclusive, daydreaming, timid, shy, and sensitive, but stubborn and self-willed, child. He still remembers with resentment how his father whipped him before another boy whom he would not thank for an apple. He was uninterested in the play life of other children and spent his time either in the town library or in his own room, where he made various toys that he guarded jealously from other children, allowing only his sister, his sole confidante, to share them. At age 17 he was graduated from high school, where he had learned easily but had taken no part in extracurricular activities.

His occupational history was without significance except that his early promise of success as a draftsman and designer of airplaines and motors had not been sustained and that for eight years prior to his commitment he had earned practically nothing. At age 20 he married.

Two months before commitment the patient began to talk about how he had failed, had "spoiled" his whole life, that it was now "too late." He spoke of hearing someone say, "You must submit." One night his wife was awakened by his talking. He told her of having several visions but refused to describe them. He stated that someone was after him and trying to blame him for the death of a certain man. He had been poisoned, he said. Whenever he saw a truck or a fire engine, the patient stated that someone in it was looking for him in order to claim his assistance to help save the world. He had periods of laughing and shouting and became so noisy and unmanageable that it was necessary to commit him.

On arrival at the hospital, the patient was noted to be an asthenic, poorly nourished man with dilated pupils, hyperactive tendon reflexes, and a pulse rate of 120 per minute. In the admission office he showed many mannerisms, lay down on the floor, pulled at his foot, made undirected violent striking movement, again struck attendants, grimaced, assumed rigid, attitudinized postures, refused to speak, and appeared to be having auditory hallucinations. He was at once placed in a continuous bath where, when seen later in the day, he was found to be in a stuporous state. His face was without expression, he was mute and rigid, and paid no attention to those about him or to their questions. His eyes were closed and the lids could be separated only with effort. There was no response to pinpricks or other painful stimuli.

On the following morning an attempt was made to bring him before the medical staff for the routine admission interview. As he was brought into the room supported by two attendants, he struggled, grimaced, shouted incoherently, and was resistive. For five days he remained mute, negativistic, and inaccessible, at times staring vacantly into space, at times with his eyes tightly closed. He ate poorly and gave no response to questions but once was heard to mutter to himself in a greatly preoccupied manner, "I'm going to die—I know it—you know it." On the evening of the sixth day he looked about, apparently astonished to find himself in the bath, and asked where he was and how he came there. When asked to tell of his life, he related many known events and how he had once worked in an airplane factory, but added that he had invented an appliance pertaining to airplanes, that this had been stolen and patented through fraud and that as a result he had lost his position. He ate ravenously, then fell asleep, and on awaking was in a catatonic stupor, remaining in this state for several days.

He gradually became accessible, and when asked concerning himself, he replied that he had had a "nervous breakdown following the physical breakdown." He referred to his stuporous period as sleep and maintained that he had no recollection of any events occuring during it. He said, "When I was in the tub I didn't know anything. Everything seemed to be dark as far as my mind is concerned. Then I began to see a little light, like the shape of a star. Then my head got through the star gradually. I saw more and more light until I saw everything in a perfect form a few days ago." Two days later he admitted that he could remember having seen the examiner while in the bath. He rationalized his former mutism by a statement that he had been afraid he would "say the wrong thing," also that he "didn't know exactly what to talk about." From his obviously inadequate emotional response and his statement that he was a "scientist and an inventor of the most extraordinary genius of the twentieth century," it was plain that he was still far from well. (A.P. Noyes and L.C. Kolb, *Modern Clinical Psychiatry*, 6th ed. Philadelphia: W.B. Saunders Co., 1963, pp. 346-7.)

In the excitement phase of catatonia, patients often show agitated activity. They may pace the floor wringing their hands, shout and yell incoherent sentences or obscenities, openly masturbate, or indulge in stereotyped automatic motions. The stereotypes may include, in addition to movements, such monotonous activities as repetitive drawings, speech, or writings. Schnauzkrampf (coined by K. I. Kahlbaum, 1828-99), a condition in which the patient protrudes the lips in a manner so that he appears to be snorting, is found almost without exception in catatonic schizophrenics.

In the agitated state, catatonics have to be watched closely. They can injure themselves severely, attempt homocide, or commit suicide. The impulsivity combined with extreme frenzy and lowered judgment can lead to a highly dangerous situation.

The following illustration is from Coleman (1964): "One patient in a frenzy of excitement gouged his left eye, and while attendants were attempting to restrain him, he managed to injure his right eye seriously."

According to the *Psychiatric Dictionary,* negativism appears in many forms:

a) external negativism, or negation of commands; *b)* innei negativism, or oppositional thoughts (actually a type of intellectual ambivalence, but often misinterpreted as "obsessive thinking"); *c)* active negativism, the active opposition of commands; *d)* passive negativism, which often appears as stubbornness or uncooperativeness; *e)* command negativism, or doing exactly the opposite of what is ordered. (Leland E. Hinsie and Robert J. Campbell, *Psychiatric Dictionary,* 3rd ed. New York: Oxford University Press, 1960, pp. 659-60.)

Prognosis is favorable in most cases of catatonic schizophrenia because onset in about 50 per cent of the reported cases is rather sudden. Electroconvulsive therapy (ECT) has been shown to be quite effective in any patient who has affective coloration involved in the total syndrome. Mood disorders are definitely included in the catatonic reaction pattern.

Hebephrenic schizophrenia is the condition the average person would associate with the "crazy" person in the "nuthouse." The most outstanding characteristic is silly, inappropriate behavior. The hebephrenic walks around, at times, with a transfixed silly grin on his face. He appears childlike in his mannerisms and will follow a stranger in the ward around like a puppy on a leash. There is a wild look in his eyes, the look that the general public identifies with mental illness.

In general, there is much alternation of behavior from wild frenzy at one time to uncontrollable crying and depression at another. Almost always, there are extreme disturbances in thought, severe agitation or blunting of emotions, and hallucinations. The delusions in this syndrome are usually illogical and center around religion, sex, health, or persecution.

The hallucinations, which generally are quite vivid, are usually auditory, the voices are convincing him that he is omnipotent, that he has changed sexes, that his insides are rotten, or that individuals or groups are out to get him. The combination of hallucinations and delusions can lead the patient to take matters into his own hands. He may try to kill the enemy or he may try homosexual seduction because of his changed sex.

Neologisms, or coined words or phrases, are common in hebephrenics. They make up words and talk in an unrelated, incoherent, bizarre manner. The following case, from Coleman, is typical:

> The patient was a divorcee, 32 years of age, who had come to the hospital with bizarre delusions, hallucinations, and severe personality disintegration with a record of alcoholism, promiscuity, and possible incestuous relations with a brother. The following conversation shows typical hebephrenic responses to questioning.
>
> Dr.: How do you feel today?
> Pt.: Fine.
> Dr.: When did you come here?
> Pt.: 1416, you remember, doctor (silly giggle).
> Dr.: Do you know why you are here?
> Pt.: Well, in 1951 I changed into two men. President Truman was judge at my trial. I was convicted and hung (silly giggle). My brother and I were given back our normal bodies five years ago. I am a policewoman. I keep a dictaphone concealed on my person.
> Dr.: Can you tell me the name of this place?
> Pt.: I have not been a drinker for sixteen years. I am taking a mental rest after a "carter" assignment or "quill." You know, a "penwrap." I had contracts with Warner Brothers Studios and Eugene broke phonograph records but Mike protested. I have been with the police department for thirty-five years. I am made of flesh and blood — see, doctor (pulling up her dress).
> Dr.: Are you married?
> Pt.: No. I am not attracted to men (silly giggle). I have a companionship arrangement with my brother. I am a "looner" . . . a bachelor. (James C. Coleman, *Abnormal Psychology and Modern Life,* 3rd ed. Chicago: Scott, Foresman & Co., 1964, pp. 278-9.)

As a group, the onset of symptoms comes earlier in hebephrenic schizophrenics (usually before twenty) than any other psychotic breakdowns. The patient has usually shown a history of bizarreness and seclusiveness. The symptoms grow progressively worse as the years pass. As a child and adolescent he is judged as strange and weird by relatives and friends. Infantile and inappropriate giggling becomes more and more frequent. When asked about the laughter, the person usually answers in an incoherent manner. Verbigeration (a senseless repetition of words) usually shows up at one point or another.

The hebephrenic reaction pattern is almost always associated with poor prognosis. As discussed previously, this could be predicted because of the gradually developing pathology and the extreme deterioration that takes place. The hebephrenic schizophrenic, once institutionalized usually remains in a mental hospital the remainder of his life.

Paranoid schizophrenia accounts for about half of the patients diagnosed as schizophrenics. The syndrome usually develops later than the other types, most patients being hospitalized between the ages of 30 and 35. As with the hebephrenic form, there has often been a history of progressive pathology. The person has been highly suspicious and generally seclusive for years before the ultimate syndrome emerges. As would be predicted, prognosis is poor in the chronic type. Paranoids, at all levels, lack trust; therefore, the therapist can easily become part of the "plot" to get the patient.

Paranoid schizophrenia combines the paranoid delusions of persecution and/or grandeur with the disturbances in thinking, autism, and emotional blunting of schizophrenia. Delusions of persecution are, by far, the most common, but most patients have several of the other types. Almost always, there are hallucinations (usually auditory) accompanying the delusions. The voices can cover the entire spectrum but some themes are more prevalent than others; for example, voices of the enemy plotting against the individual, the voice of God, voices discussing sexual "filth," or voices telling the patient to commit some act of violence or self-destruction.

As a rule, the delusions and hallucinations are illogical, incoherent, bizarre, and lack the consistency of delusions of paranoia. The patient may think he is Christ, Napoleon, or Mary. One patient in a nearby mental hospital says that he is one of the two living prophets of God. The previously cited case, in the discussion on delusions, was diagnosed as a paranoid schizophrenic. If two or more Christs end up in the same institution, the situation can become quite interesting (c.f. *The Three Christs of Ypsilanti,* Rokeach, 1964).

Some paranoid schizophrenic reactions are acute and can be cleared up in a short period of time if proper therapy is given. The following case, is of this type.

The case to be reported occured in a 41-year-old command pilot with 7,500 hours, who had flown 135 combat missions in World War II and Korea. At the time of his illness, he was a chief pilot in a command headquarters. He was an excellent pilot and had consistently received superior ratings because of his conscientious and dependable performance. The overt onset of his illness was related to a period of TDY at a conference where flight procedures on a new type aircraft were being drafted. However, in retrospect, it was learned that for several weeks he had been preoccupied and upset, had sensed that he could read other people's minds by radio waves, and suspected those with whom he worked of being 'queer.'

While at the conference, he developed ideas of reference, believing that certain comments which his companions made, or which he heard over the radio, had hidden meanings and were directed toward him. For example, when the conferees spoke of "take-off," he did not know whether they were referring to an airplane or a woman, and suspected they were suggesting he should have an illicit sexual relationship. He developed the delusional idea that his associates were trying to "teach" him something, and puzzled them several times when he confronted them with a demand that they tell him openly whatever they wanted him to learn. They became further concerned when he became increasingly upset, tearful and incoherent, and when he did not improve after several days of "rest" at his brother's home, he was admitted to the hospital.

On admission, he was suspicious of those about him, wondering whether they were dope-peddlers or communists, and he refused to talk to people who could not assure him they were cleared for top secret. He believed that he was accused of taking dope, that there were concealed microphones about the ward, and he had hallucinations consisting of voices which accused him of being "queer." He was often apprehensive and tearful, but this alternated with periods when he was inappropriately jovial. He was oriented in all spheres and physical and neurological exams were entirely normal.

A review of the patient's past history revealed no other evidence of emotional disturbance. He was the second of four children of a strict, moralistic, financially successful farm family. He did well in school and one year of college, but always felt inadequate in comparison with his peers. He entered the Air Corps and flew 32 B-17 missions in World War II, was separated, then recalled in 1950 and flew 103 combat missions in Korea. He had been married for 18 years and had five children. He used alcohol only rarely, and there was no evidence that toxic or exogenous factors could have been implicated in his psychosis.

The patient received psychotherapy and began to improve within a few days after admission. For this reason, no drug or other somatic treatment was instituted. He continued to improve over the course of the next several weeks and seemed greatly relieved after telling of an isolated extramartial adventure during the TDY. He gradually gained insight into the unreality of his experiences and was discharged from the hospital after one month.

Following his discharge, the patient was given duties in supply and ground training which he handled without difficulty. However, he had always enjoyed flying immensely and taken pride in his outstanding proficiency, and he made repeated visits to his flight surgeon and psychiatrist to try to get back on flying status. He was referred to the School of Aerospace Medicine for evaluation and recommendations regarding return to flying status.

When seen at the school, he was found to be very well integrated, although some underlying anxiety was apparent. Despite his apparently satisfactory remission, some residuals of his previous thinking disorder were evident. He wondered at times whether he had not been partly right about the events on TDY, and whether his fellow conferees had not been playing a practical joke on him. He had recently considered going to his Wing Commanding Officer to ask whether the experiences had been part of some kind of "test" of his mental stability, but had decided against this because it might create an unfavorable impression if he were being tested. He had decided that whatever had happened, it was best forgotten, and through the use of this suppressive mechanism had continued to function effectively. Because of his clear-cut history of a psychotic disorder without an underlying organic basis, as well as the evidence of a continuing minimal thinking disorder, return to flying status was not considered to be consistent with flying safety. (L. J. Enders and D. E. Flinn, "Clinical Problems in Aviation Medicine—Schizophrenic Reaction, Paranoid Type," *Aerospace Medicine,* vol. 33, 1962, pp. 730-1.)

The psychoanalytic view of paranoia in all its forms is that the condition is largely due to projected latent homosexuality. A large segment of the personality has been repressed and there is a continual battle being waged internally. There is a constant threat of exposure not only to others but to oneself. The person cannot trust his own impulses, so how can he trust anyone else? This conflict is largely handled by projection, that is, "It is not I who feel this way; it is those other people who are trying to corrupt me." There is some experimental evidence to support this Freudian viewpoint, for example Moore and Selzer (1963).

The other forms of schizophrenia will not be discussed in this book for two reasons: (1) there is a chance of confusing the reader, and (2) the incidence of these types is rare. For the interested reader, other forms can be checked out in standard textbooks in abnormal psychology or psychiatry. Some of the other types are: (1) childhood, (2) acute undifferentiated, (3) chronic undifferentiated, (4) schizo-affective, (5) residual, (6) pseudoneurotic, (7) pseudopsychopathic, and (8) ambulatory.

Paranoid reactions

There are two paranoid reactions other than paranoid schizophrenia, namely, paranoia (the paranoid personality) and the paranoid state. The use of the word paranoia has a long history. It was used by the Greeks and Romans to designate any mental illness. The current definition of delusions of persecution and/or grandeur comes from Kraepelin.

The paranoid personality is characterized by highly systematized and logical delusions. If others accept his basic assumption, everything the paranoid says makes sense. The problem is that the basic premise (usually about plots or conspiracies) is false. In the 1964 election year, a flood of paranoid books about "communist plots" hit the market. These books are perfectly logical and well presented if one assumes that everyone is a communist or communist dupe "except me and thee."

This leads to the point that there is probably some paranoia in all of us. Other people let us down or trouble seems to come in bunches. We know that we do not always tell the truth, so why should we trust the motives of others? We know that they place self-interest above altruism. A clever paranoid or unfortunate events can aggravate this mistrust in us quite easily.

Paranoia, prejudice, and authoritarianism are closely related. All three are based upon a threat orientation toward life. The new, different, unusual, or unknown produces discomfort because of separation anxiety. The only way to reduce threat is to have "law and order." This, in turn, leads to a power orientation. "Might makes right" becomes the personal philosophy of these suspicious individuals. Man is seen as inherently evil; therefore, the only way to keep him in line is to force him to be good. This can be accomplished only through power and order.

Paranoids are attracted to politics; two paranoid personalities of this century, Hilter and Stalin, were directly or indirectly responsible for the death of 50 million people. Politics satisfies the power and order drives. In addition, it gives the person a chance to project and externalize.

The paranoid is unaware of many of his motives; unacceptable motives are repressed, and in turn, attributed to others. Things don't happen inside the person, they happen "out there." If the evil forces are "out there," then it is perfectly logical to fight against them. Anything new or different is a threat; it must be resisted. The state is all important; the individual must adjust his needs and wishes to the structure.

Invariably, the demagogue resorts to emotionally-loaded symbols, such as God, mother and country. He knows the value of agitating the paranoid feelings in his audience. Anyone who expresses opinions opposed to his is a threat to these sacred symbols. Consequently, he must be dealt with firmly and harshly or "law and order" will collapse. Too, such evil people will lead the masses into moral decadence.

Not all paranoid delusions involve international or national conspiracies. They may center around a single person such as a mother-in-law or wife, or a small group such as neighbors, relatives, colleagues, or the congregation of a church. The following is an example:

> Milner cited the case of a paranoiac, aged 33, who murdered his wife by battering her head with a hammer. Prior to the murder, he had become convinced that his wife was suffering from some strange disease and that she had purposely infected him because she wished him to die. He believed that this disease was due to a 'cancer-consumption' germ. He attributed his conclusion in part to his wife's alleged sexual perversion and also gave the following reasons for his belief:
> 1. His wife had insured him for a small sum immediately after marriage.
> 2. A young man who had been friendly with his wife before their marriage died suddenly.
> 3. A child who had lived in the same house as his wife's parents suffered from fits. (He also believed that his wife's parents were suffering from the same disease.)
> 4. For several months before the crime his food had had a queer taste, and for a few weeks before the crime he had suffered from a pain in the chest and an unpleasant taste in the mouth. (K. O. Milner, "The Environment as a Factor in the Aetiology of Criminal Paranoia," *Journal of Mental Science,* vol. 95, 1949, p. 130.)

As with all delusions, the paranoiac will steadfastly maintain his belief in spite of logical contradiction or evidence to the contrary. Often, the person will take a minor incident and blow it up into huge proportions. This type of paranoid reaction often precedes the final psychotic breakdown in advanced alcoholism. The so-called "alcoholic jealousy" is essentially a delusion not only of persecution but also of infidelity. The mate is accused of adultery and of attempts to conspire against the alcoholic. Paranoid delusions are also quite frequent in catatonics in the period just preceding the first episode.

Paranoid states differ from paranoia in two important ways: 1) they are usually of a transitory nature and 2) the delusions are less systematized. The syndrome is intermediate between paranoia and paranoid schizophrenia. The person shows the disorientation, emotional blunting, disturbances in thought processes and bizarreness of the schizophrenic but the symptoms often disappear with or without therapy. This disappearance, of course, indicates that this condition may be situationally induced. There may be a kernel of truth in the paranoid attitudes and as soon as the environment changes, the person changes.

Most cases are acute, that is, there is a sudden appearance of symptoms, and the episode can be precipitated by a traumatic experience. But some people go on to develop either full-blown paranoid attitudes or the paranoid schizophrenic withdrawal pattern.

Paranoid personalities and some persons in the paranoid state frequently stay in the community and avoid institutionalization. When this happens they can bring havoc into the lives of their friends and relatives. For example, poison-pen letters have been known to fragment a group to the point that reconciliation becomes impossible. The paranoid seed, once planted, can grow like a weed. It can take over a person's mental life in a short period of time.

Affective disorders

Everyone has moods. There are times when we are

elated and times when we are depressed. The affective psychotic reactions are exaggerations of these basic moods. The two major types of affective disorders are *a)* manic-depressive reactions and *b)* mixed reactions (sometimes called agitated depression). Affective components are often found in other psychotic reactions.

The term manic-depressive is hyphenated because the patient usually goes from one side of the mood continuum to the other, though some people show the manic reaction only or the depression only. Depressive reactions are much more common than are manic reactions. There are three levels of psychotic manic reactions, graded from a mild to a severe psychotic breakdown, namely, hypomania, acute mania, and delirious mania.

Hypomania, on the surface, resembles our state of being on those days we have when "it is great to be alive." It is characterized by overactivity, elation, euphoria, and pleasant excitability. It differs from normal elation in that contact with reality is lowered. There is usually a wild flight of ideas.

The individual may come up with many grandiose plans and schemes, but there is a discontinuity between the ideas and within the thought processes. He becomes unable to sit still or concentrate for any length of time. He shows restless hyperactivity and little patience for monotony or the mundane. If he wishes to get in touch with someone, standard mail service is much too slow. He will send a telegram or make a long distance call. Several manics have tried to wire, call, or personally contact the President of the United States with some grandiose plan for the nation.

At first glance, the manic appears to be a highly energetic, dynamic person. His enthusiasm and apparent brilliance can astound a group briefly. Then, it rapidly becomes apparent that his ideas are disconnected and disoriented. He is often overbearing and uncouth. He may show total disrespect for the rights or ideas of others. He has a tendency to try to take over, whether it be in conversation or action.

Moral inhibitions are lowered, so that he tends to indulge in previously prohibited behavior. He may become obscene in his language, indiscreet in making sexual advances, or promiscuous. Alcohol is frequently used to keep the condition going. The person may go for days without sleep. Often he will continue until he becomes totally physically exhausted.

A common form of manic episode employs religious conversion as the basic instrument. The person may quote verse after verse from the Bible and try to "save" everyone he can contact. He may indulge in frenzied activity such as rolling around on the floor or "talking in tongues," or he may go into bars to try to convert the sinners. However, even when the religious overtones are present, the person shows gross inconsistencies in thought and behavior. He may string obscenities into the Biblical quotations or make openly seductive advances while he is preaching. These sexual advances can be heterosexual, homosexual, or bisexual.

The author attended a tent revival service once in which a woman was rolling around in the sawdust and "talking in tongues." During this episode the hem of her skirt crept up to her waistline. One discreet member of the congregation attempted to pull the skirt down. The revivalist shouted to this man, "Glory be to God, Brother, leave her alone. Let her glory shine."

Delusions and hallucinations are not common in manic episodes, though they do occur, especially in the religious variety where the vision quest is encouraged. Even when these elements are not present, the individual shows little or no insight into his condition. Any suggestion that he might be ill is met with active resistance and, often, open aggression. This is an example of hypomania:

> The patient, a 50-year-old female, was brought to the hospital in an acute manic state but through the use of drugs had been brought down to hypomania by the time of the following.
>
> An interview was conducted before an audience of student nurses and college psychology students. During the interview, the patient would remain seated only a few minutes, then would get up and wander about. She responded to many of the psychiatrist's questions with Biblical quotations. She told all of the students what sinners they were and encouraged them to "be born again." Between the preaching, she was making openly seductive advances to male and female alike. She would lift her dress and wink at one of the students. At one point, she charged into the audience and began to caress one of the nurses.
>
> During the interview, she stated that the Holy Ghost had brought her a pair of stockings over the weekend while her husband and son were away from home. That was when she had been "saved." And now that she had been "reborn" she wanted all the students to have the same experience.

Acute mania and delirious mania, the more advanced forms of manic reactions, are merely more pronounced excitement symptoms. In acute mania, the individual is irritable and easily provoked and he may become violent. Motor restlessness is prominent. The individual may pace, or even run, back and forth, making all sorts of automatic gestures and verbalizations. Not too many years ago, acute manic patients were placed in padded cells in straight jackets for their own protection and for the safety of others. Their frenzied activity can lead to serious injury. Today, acute manics and delirious manics are largely controlled through the use of drugs.

In acute manic episodes there is usually a wild flight of ideas which are disconnected and disoriented. Thought and speech become incoherent. It is impossible to keep up with the rapid jumps from one idea or action to the next. The erotic-religious mixture of thoughts and actions is common in this reaction, as it is in hypomania, but the symptoms are more pronounced.

Delusions and hallucinations may occur but they usually are short-lived and show little or no continuity. When these conditions do appear, the elements are usually grandiose.

Delirious mania is the condition associated in popular language with the "raving lunatic." The patient runs around screaming and yelling at the top of his lungs and may be quite dangerous to himself or others. He shows no contact with reality. He may tear his clothes off, smear feces on himself, the walls, or on others, or violently smash everything in sight. Vivid hallucinations and delusions are common. The wild-eyed gaze popularly associated with mental illness is quite evident.

One acceptable explanation of the manic reaction is that it is a defense against depression. In essence, this behavior is an exaggerated suppressive technique. Suppression has been called a flight into reality. Mania serves the same purpose but could be described as a flight into activity. The central idea seems to be one of staying extremely busy and active so that one does not have to think about himself or his troubles.

Some patients start with hypomania and progress to delirious mania, but most cases involve a sudden onset of symptoms. Consequently, prognosis is favorable with or without therapy. However, without treatment, most patients will have other mania attacks at some later date.

Depressive reactions are universal, unpleasant facts

of life. Everyone feels depressed at times, and this mental state covers the entire spectrum from normal, through neurotic, to psychotic depression.

Normal depression involves a general slowing down, both physically and mentally. The person usually develops self-derogatory and self-depreciating attitudes. In Freudian terms, depression is the result of moral anxiety and the products are guilt and shame. All of us have these feelings from time to time, but we can overcome them in a reasonable period of time. In neurotic depression the symptoms are about the same, perhaps more exaggerated, but they are prolonged for indefinite periods and saturate the person's life. Usually, neurotic depression is precipitated by a traumatic episode in the individual's life, for example, death, divorce, or material loss.

There are three levels of psychotic depressions: simple depression, acute depression, and depressive stupor. As with mania, the levels show increasing pathology along a continuum. Simple depression is not too distant from normal depression. There is a physical and mental slowing down. The person feels down in the dumps. He has no enthusiasm for anything and expending energy requires great effort. Even eating and listening to others may become chores. He does everything in slow motion, from lighting a cigarette to trying to talk. If the person does talk, the conversation is usually in a low-pitched monotone, and there may be long pauses between words.

His mental attitude is one of self-depreciation. The person feels that he has sinned, is wicked and evil, and often, that he would be doing others a favor if he were to end it all. The future looks dim because nothing good can come of anything he does. Because he is so evil, he prefers to sit alone and think his morbid thoughts. He wants to sit and indulge in self-pity or to be punished for his awful behavior. The individual becomes extremely self-centered but usually in a derogatory manner.

In spite of the apparent loss of concern with the environment, in simple depression most patients are in touch and may even have some insight into their problems, but they don't know what to do about the situation. The physical slowing down leads to loss of interest in food and beverages. Consequently, physical deterioration and health factors may enter in and complicate the situation. The loss of stamina and general appearance of fatigue have often led to an improper diagnosis of neurasthenia. Delusions and hallucinations are rare in simple depression. The patient usually feels that he is being punished or should be punished for some unworthy act or acts.

Acute depression is an exaggeration of simple depression. There is an even greater amount of physical and mental slowing down. The patient sits, stares off into space, and is not likely to respond to the conversation of others. If he does respond, his conversation is generally in an extremely weak monotone with prolonged pauses between words and phrases. The feelings of guilt, shame, and worthlessness are even more pronounced than in simple depression. Morbid thoughts about sex, sin, death, health, and especially suicide occupy the entire consciousness of the person.

Nihilistic and hypochondriacal delusions become much more prevalent at this level. The patient may feel that he is living in a shadow world, or that he is a hollow shell. He sometimes thinks that his entire insides are rotting or that his guts have turned to sawdust. These horrible conditions are often related to earlier masturbation or other "sinful" sex practices. Some hallucinations have been reported at this level. These visions relate to the delusions in that they, too, center around unacceptable impulses, sin, and evilness.

In depressive stupor, the patient remains totally immobile, quite often bedridden. He responds to nothing that is going on around him, not even food or drink. Usually, the person has to be fed intravenously and someone has to take care of excretory processes. Vivid hallucinations and bizarre delusions centering around the morbid are usually reported. In fact, it is to these phenomena that the patient is attending. He is listening to the voices talking about filth, death, and sinful acts. His delusions about himself are merely an exaggeration of the false beliefs at the acute depression level.

At all levels of depression, suicide is a possibility. This is especially true in psychotic depression. The person must be kept under close observation or mood-elevating drugs must be used.

As with mania, depression will work itself off in time, with or without psychotherapy (that is, if the person does not kill himself.) However, without treatment, the probability of recurrence is high. ECT (electroconvulsive therapy) has been highly successful in bringing about a termination of depressive symptoms, but if recidivism is to be prevented, the ECT should be combined with psychotherapy before the patient is released.

Agitated depression is a syndrome in which the patient shows the physical symptoms of mania and the mental symptoms of depression. The patient may pace back and forth, wringing his hands expressing all sorts of morbid ideas of sin, death, and rebirth. Usually, the individual fears that his sins have been so great that not only he, but his loved ones are going to be punished. The physical overactivity grows out of the excitement engendered by this fear of punishment. Agitated depression normally occurs in conjunction with the involutional disorders (to be discussed next) but is occasionally found in preinvolutional persons.

A few cases of manic stupor have been reported. In this condition, the person sits in a stuporous position but there is a wild flight of elated or euphoric ideas.

Involutional psychosis is the appearance of psychotic symptoms in later life with no previous history of psychotic behavior. The word involutional refers to regression in the later years as opposed to the evolution of earlier years. The involutional period of life generally includes the age ranges forty to fifty-five for women and fifty to sixty-five for men.

Involutional melancholia is most often associated with women and usually occurs in conjunction with the menopause. It normally includes symptoms that resemble agitated depression. The person becomes moody, anxious, and irritable. Insomnia and worry are prevalent. The woman may burst into tears with little or no provocation. These preliminary symptoms have sometimes been called "the menopause syndrome."

Later, the patient develops the full-scale agitated depression symptoms of extreme worry and dread about impending doom, suffering, and punishment. Hypochondriacal and nihilistic delusions often enter into the total syndrome. Many persons complicate the situation even more by turning to alcohol. As in any case of depression, suicide becomes an imminent possibility.

Involutional paranoia is the appearance of paranoid symptoms in the later years with no previous history of paranoia. If paranoid delusions do occur, early hospitalization is imperative, because some persons have been known to try to take matters into their own hands; acts of violence may be committed against the "persecutors," even if these tormentors happen to be members of the immediate family.

Senility is included by some authorities as one of the involutional disorders. The word senility means old age, but is more commonly associated with "the second childhood," or the stubbornness, cantankerousness, irritability, tendency to reminisce (living in the past) and emotional instability of the aged.

The older people grow, the greater the likelihood of their becoming institutionalized, whether they are truly psychotic or whether they are merely judged as weird and bizarre by their relatives and friends. Growing old in a youth-oriented society is not easy. Reflecting back on one's accomplishments (with possible concern over failure) is never as satisfying as the hopes, ambitions, and plans of youth. It is little wonder that high percentages of the aged in the United States develop some symptoms that could be called abnormal.

references

Adorno, T. W., Frenkel-Brunswik, E., Levinson, D. J., & Sanford, R. N. *The authoritarian personality.* New York: Harper, 1950.

Allport, G. W. *The nature of prejudice.* New York: Anchor, 1958.

Bluemel, C. S. *War, politics, and insanity.* Denver: World Press, 1948.

Blum, R., et al. *Utopiates.* New York: Atherton, 1965.

Coleman, J. C. *Abnormal psychology and modern life.* (3rd ed). Chicago: Scott, Foresman and Co., 1964.

Davis, G. (Ed.) *The story,* vol. 3, no. 3, Fall, 1966.

Enders, L. J. & Flinn, D. E. Clinical problems in aviation medicine. Schizophrenic reaction, paranoid type. *Aerospace Medicine,* 33, 1962.

Erikson, E. H. *Childhood and society.* New York: Norton, 1950.

Freud, S. *Leonardo da Vinci: A study in psychosexuality.* New York: Random House, 1947.

———. *Totem and taboo* (1913). *In collected papers of*.... New York: Basic Books, 1959.

———. *The future of an illusion* (1927). New York: Anchor, 1964.

Glasser, W. *Reality therapy.* New York: Harper & Row, 1965.

Goldfarb, W. Effects of psychological deprivation in infancy and subsequent stimulation. *American Journal of Psychiatry,* 102, 1945.

Harlow, H. F. Affectional behavior in the infant monkey. In Brazier, M. A. B. (Ed.) *Central nervous system and behavior.* New York: Josia Macy, Jr. Foundation, 1962.

Hinsie, L. E. & Campbell, R. J. *Psychiatric dictionary* (3rd ed.) New York: Oxford University Press, 1960.

Hubbard, L. R. *Dianetics.* New York: Hermitage House, 1950.

Huxley, A. *Brave new world.* New York: Harper & Row, 1932.

———. *The doors of perception.* New York: Harper & Row, 1963.

———. *Heaven and hell.* New York: Harper & Row, 1963.

Kant, O. Clinical investigation of simple schizophrenia. *Psychiatric Quarterly,* 22, 1948.

Karpman, B. The psychopathology of exhibitionism. *Journal of Clinical Psychopathy,* 9, 179-225, 1948.

Kennedy, F., Hoffman, H. R., & Haines, W. H. A study of William Heirens. *American Journal of Psychiatry,* 104, 113-21, 1947.

Kinsey, A. C., Pomeroy, W. B., & Martin, C. E. *Sexual behavior in the human male.* Philadelphia: W. B. Saunders, 1948.

———. *Sexual behavior in the human female.* Philadelphia: W. B. Saunders, 1953.

Kraines, S. H. *Therapy of the neuroses and psychoses* (3rd ed.) Philadelphia: Lea & Febiger, 1948.

Lindner, R. *Must you conform?* New York: Grove Press, 1956.

Lion, E. G., Jambor, Helen M., Corrigan, Hazel G., & Bradway, Katherine P. *An experiment in the psychiatric treatment of promiscuous girls.* San Francisco: Department of Public Health, 1945.

Masserman, J. H. *Principle of dynamic psychiatry* (2nd ed.) Philadelphia: Saunders, 1961.

———. Report to the Council of the American Psychiatric Association, Oct. 29, 1966. *American Psychiatric Association News,* Jan., 1967.

Milner, K. O. The environment as a factor in the aetiology of criminal paranoia. *Journal of Mental Science,* 95, 1949.

Moore, R. A. & Selzer, M. L. Male homosexuality, paranoia, and the schizophrenias. *American Journal of Psychiatry* 119, 1963.

Noyes, A. P. & Kolb, L. C. *Modern Clinical Psychiatry* (6th ed.) Philadelphia: W. B. Saunders, 1963.

Nyswander, Marie. Drug addictions. In Arieti, S. (Ed.) *American handbook of psychiatry,* Vol. 1. New York: Basic Books, 1959.

Osnos, R. J. The treatment of narcotics addiction. *New York Journal of Medicine,* 63, 1963.

Ribble, Margaret A. Clinical studies of instinctive reactions in newborn babies. *American Journal of Psychiatry,* 95, 1938.

Rokeach, M. *The three Christs of Ypsilanti.* New York: Knopf, 1964.

Seevers, M. H. Medical perspectives on habituation and addiction. *Journal of American Medical Association,* 181, 1962.

Selye, H. *The Stress of Life.* New York: McGraw-Hill, 1956.

Sherman, M. *Mental conflicts and personality.* New

York: Longmans, Green, & Co., 1938.

Skinner, B. F. *Science and human behavior.* New York: Macmillan, 1953.

Spitz, R. A. *The first year of life; a psychoanalytic study of normal and deviant development of object relations.* New York: McGraw-Hill, 1957.

Thigpen, C. H. & Cleckly, H. M. *Three faces of Eve.* New York: McGraw-Hill, 1957.

Thorndike, E. L *Animal intelligence.* New York: Macmillan, 1911.

————. *The fundamentals of learning.* New York: Teachers College of Columbia University, 1932.

Thorpe, L. P., Katz, B., & Lewis, R. T. *The psychology of abnormal behavior.* New York: Ronald, 1961.

Trainer, P. *The Lolita complex.* New York: The Cita del Press, 1966.

Wertham, F. *The show of violence.* New York: Doubleday, 1949.

index